My Journey To A #SizeSatisfied & Finding Me In The Process

Losing the Weight of My Worries

Dedication:

**To All Who Aim
To Conquer Life's Struggles**

#GodIsntFinishedWithMeYet
#TheUniverseIsntFinishedWithMeYet

My Journey To A #SizeSatisfied & Finding Myself In the Process

Losing the Weight of My Worries

My Journey To A #SizeSatisfied

Hello, my name is Regina Hardy. I am a single mother of three beautiful girls, 2 amazing grandchildren and the owner of a very energetic dog. My children are 14, 23 and 24 with my granddaughter being 8 and my grandson being 4. Bailey the dog is 2.

I live in the suburbs of New York City. I live in Nassau County, Long Island. I work a full time job or several part time jobs. Both ways I work and I work hard. I follow my passions yet and still I struggle to make ends meet in life. I have a child in culinary school, a child out trying to find her own, a child in high school, and a granddaughter I have custody of. My grandson for now is staying with another family member which causes a constant battle of trying to keep siblings together. Does this sound like the "normal" family set up or composition? The diversity only gets better. Please let's keep reading. There are so many differences in each one of our lives yet so much is the same.

I have bills out the wahzoo. To the point where I sometimes sneak up on my house after work to see if the outside sensor light will come on. This way I know if my electric is still on or if it was shut off. Better yet, how about waking up in the middle of the night to use the bathroom or get some water and you glance over to the cable box and you have those famous four dashes across the front or the message scrolling across that reads "Please contact your local cable provider for service". Or attempting to make a call on your cell and you immediately get rerouted to customer service because your service has been interrupted. Let's go for the icing and the cherry on the cake. How about when you hear a truck outside your house and it's backing up, BEEP BEEP BEEP BEEP. You hold your breath because you're not sure if it's parking. So you close your eyes and pray it's not the repo to pick up your car because you're late on a payment or two or utility company because you fell behind on your payment agreement.

Yup that type of life. I am here to tell you all that yes I am about that life. Yes, the life where I can't believe I work so hard to be so broke. Yet I know and feel as though there is something greater and amazing just around the corner. It's so close I can just about taste the aroma. I know I am not alone and I know that trouble don't last always. So with my eyes on the prize and passion in my heart I know that life is so amazing!

Please don't get me wrong, I still at times get upset. I may even still yell and scream. There are times even that my mouth can be a little on the vulgar side. However, that doesn't mean I am not happier with my life now than I was before.

I just think and breathe before I act or speak when I am upset. I work on me and with me in midst of it all. As I have learned that life is a process I know I am a work in progress. Be assured that still I smile because I truly know my life is Amazing.

I want to share with you the way to that amazing feeling so please just come with me on this little journey. I hope it inspires, motivates or guides someone in a way that it improves your life and the way you see things. If that doesn't happen like all who have met me and not been on this ride from the beginning be ready to either be baffled or entertained. Just know that had I not lived this I wouldn't believe it was one person's life either.

I have overcome so much more than what my current situations are; so much that my current situation is nothing more than a ripple in the waves of my life. I want to use this time to shed some light on one of my biggest hurdles in my life: my weight.

2

I'd like to share things that I encountered that caused me to gain it and what I did to lose it. I use to weigh close to 400 lbs. Yes 400 lbs! Last time I approached the scale at that time I was approximately 367 lbs. Believe it or not I really didn't even know that my weight had gotten away from me like that.

I was so blind to what was going on with me because I had lost myself in my situations and circumstances. I needed to take control and get my weight and my life together. I wasn't doing it to be vain or for vanity purposes. I was on this journey to a #SizeSatisfied for health reasons. Let me continue and I'll explain a little further.

I mean I knew that I was a plus size woman, I just didn't realize how "plus size" I was. When I took the time to see what I was doing to my life I had to take control. I had allowed life to get in the way and I forgot to take care of me.

Before I take you through what I did to take control of my life and my weight let's just briefly run through a few of the curve balls life was throwing at me from early childhood up until now. Just some, not many and most definitely not all. I want to get this out to you, my readers, so that you too can begin your journey, your healing process, looking at things from a new perspective or whatever else you get outof this great read.

During my early childhood I was raised in a single family home on Long Island, pretty low income family. We may have been poor when it came to money however we were rich with love, laughter and memories. I was what I thought to be a pretty average child. Average in the sense that I did kid things school, play, eat and sleep for the most part. Until life had plans to show me things I didn't even think was in my future.

Have you ever felt like the ugly duckling, the black sheep, the one everyone forgets about until something is needed or they needed someone to blame things on, well that was me. Always feeling as though you are not good enough, like you fit in nowhere, as if you're a total misfit? Well if not, lucky you. I have felt that way most of my life. I know they say that misery loves company just know I never met nor did I ever find company. Lord knows I was miserable.

I have no problem admitting that now, for I've come to crossroad where I know better so I do better. Since I have chosen this route I most definitely feel better. I do what's best for me in my situations not what's best suggested by those who can't fathom my situation. I take in positivity and attempt to brush off negativity. Don't get me wrong it isn't easy yet it is a very necessary process. It requires practice just as anything else in life you've ever learned.

Study, patience, practice, practice and more practice. You too deserve peace in your life take time for you to find out what you need in your life. Always be true and real with yourself and you'll find out just how natural it comes to be this way with the world. In order to achieve greatness you must first believe and practice greatness. You can manifest whatever you desire in your life you just have to will it into existence.

Things aren't always as bad they as they seem. Know and believe that any situation can always be worse. There are always going to be dark times until you are open to seeing the light. Get out of your own way! I know I had to get out of mine.

I grew up with friends who became family such as aunts, uncles, cousins as well as really close friends being considered brothers and sisters. Granted in my home growing up we loved each other as younger siblings. As time passed we grew up and apart now we don't really get along. Honestly, I am a bit clueless as to why we don't quite see eye to eye. Yet there are times in life you just have to learn to walk away. Not because you don't care about them, more so because you care about yourself much more. I've heard a very wise man say "Blood makes you relative and Love makes you family."

The negative feelings or thoughts that you allow to enter your mind soon can take over your body. The physically problems can range from headaches, sweats, heart palpitations, shortness of breath, rage, anger and so much more. If it gets too bad and out of hand, we may even act out on these feelings with actions we can't take back with lessons we could've learned simply without the actual experience.

Like a campfire, negativity can spark a wildfire. Be in control of your thoughts and actions. Yes, I know that's easier said than done yet once again practice, practice and more practice. Like the sport you learned and love the new language you've picked up, the recipe you have perfected. Put as much love and work into yourself as you do into the people and things around you. You'll be surprised at the results you'll get out. Before you know it you will gain a special gift at high levels called confidence.

Build your self-confidence and promote the reflection of you that you want to shine and be noticed. You are golden and are chosen. You have a purpose in this life, here on this Earth; make your presence count. You are a gift and you possess a gift be sure to share that with the world and leave your best impression. Many may not understand and begin to call you cocky. You're not being cocky by any means, you must continue to radiate with confidence as you walk through life. Don't allow anyone to dull your shine once you've found your inner sparkle.

I've always been afraid of my capabilities. I'd always second guess myself; my self-doubt screamed loud obscenities. It felt as though acceptance was far from a guarantee, it felt like "it" was just never going to happen in life. Yet regardless of how low I'd feel there was always something deeper in me telling me that things would get better and brighter. So I held on to that feeling which I later found out was called hope. I took that glimpse of hope and just kept the faith as I went on daily with this process of life. I continued to focus on the dim light that I felt from time to time.

That's all you need is a little something positive and direct to focus on. Why not let it be you. All things that are going on around will always be there. They are only as important as the life you give it. Give yourself life and relevance. You need no one's approval. Be you. Be weird, be funny, be fabulous, be different, be broke, be in charge, be rich, be focused, be determined, be motivated, be positive... Be whatever example you wish you ever had and then set an example for someone else. Let's not be selfish.

3

I have an older sister and a younger brother; I am the middle child of my mother's three children. There always seemed to be this tension between me and my mother's first born. I mean I will not apologize for being born that was never a choice for me. However, I appreciate the fact that I beat over 5 billion sperm cells and I have a purpose here on Earth in this life.

Seriously, I can't go around trying to save the world and figure out all the answers to life's hidden secrets. I have attempted on many occasions to mend the ripple however I always get the door slammed in face. There are times in life when you have to learn what doors are worth kicking down and which ones to turn and walk away from. Know that sometimes in life, choices are made for you it's just up to you to follow through.

Growing up in a single parent household, for the most part, was pretty normal for me. I mean I did it and many friends in my neighborhood did it too. There were just some things that seemed to be the norm. Even when things seemed so out of pocket and so farfetched some people just looked at it like it was "normal" so what was I do as a child. From seeing drug deals and raids, fights with machetes and knives, attempted and successful sexual assaults and fiends that had to beg, rob and steal to support their habits. My daily sights were just as adventurous as today's reality TV shows.

I dealt with being molested as a child by a so-called "family friend". You know that uncle that wasn't really your uncle. Yup, that good ole uncle that would take me out for ice cream and "driving lessons". Yeah I'd scream alright. Problem was the people I told didn't seem to believe me. I'd say I didn't want to go and I was told it was okay. I hated going for these "driving lessons" down at the local baseball field behind the ice cream shop. That's probably why I stay away from visiting back home to this day. Now memories I would love to erase haunt me with sights that will never disappear. These events changed me as a child and stalked me into adulthood. I was only between the ages of 8-10 give or take.

My moods would change and I was angry at the world. I trusted no one and nothing. I never felt protected or as though I'd ever be able to be loved. These issues have plagued me for so many years. They came with me from my childhood right into adulthood. There were these times I'd be upset and crying or just feel enraged for what appeared to me as no reason at all at that moment. Now I realize it was something that would trigger my sensory organs and a memory subconsciously would take over.

Many times I couldn't put my finger on it. I couldn't understand what my frustration stemmed from. My anger was coming out of me as rebellious actions and being a bit defiant at times. This festered and grew over the years. I became withdrawn for a time then I became a bit promiscuous. I began to look for the wrong "qualities" in people to find my mate whether it was for the moment or a lifetime. I did all types of things for the wrong types of attention.

4

I was attracted to the streets so guess what type of dudes I would attract. Yup you got it - street. Thugged out, hustlers, drug dealers etc etc. Let's just say the lifestyle could be so full of adventure from one moment to the next. Never really knew if I'd be ducking bullets and glass bottles, running and hopping fences or high speed car chases with people waving guns out of the windows. Attending house parties where people would have fights and get beaten to a bloody pulp and left in the bushes to be cleaned up later. This was more than I even imagined. However due to choices I made this was the life that I lived then. Young teen running wild doing what I wanted when I wanted as though nothing else mattered; boy oh boy too many that may sound all too familiar.

When I was a young 15 year old, my mother got incarcerated. I was distraught. I didn't know what to think or how to feel. I recall going back and forth to court and visits to the county jail where all the women were wearing forest green jumpsuits or what resembled scrubs to me. Then all the male inmates that came down to visiting room would be wearing bright orange jumpsuits or scrubs.

It was dark and dreary in that visiting room. I recall walking through the metal detectors. Being told to remove all layers of clothes, all your jewelry, your shoes, hair pins out of your hair (Lord save you if you had a wig or a weave with pins), no gum or candy in your mouth, gates opening and slamming, correctional officers on mics talking behind thick plated glass... The list goes on and on and on. Some memories truly don't just fade away.

I eventually got pregnant. My first pregnancy ended in a miscarriage during a fight. I was simply defending myself in a bully type situation. I was devastated to find out that I lost the baby let alone that I was even pregnant. I was only 15 years old. I wasn't sure who to speak to let alone what to say, so I told only the baby's father and lived with this pain for years.

Shortly thereafter I began dating a different man who was older than I was and that wasn't the wisest of choices. Yet in that moment it was the best thing that I wanted to do. After dating him for a few months I found out that I was once again pregnant. I was determined to have my baby, love her, protect her and care for her for the rest of my life. There was nothing or no one that was going to stop this from happening.

That was the straw that began to break the camel's back. Family became rude and disrespectful. Their actions and words toward me stayed with me for life. I know that I may have been young however I had already endured so much in life no one was aware of what I felt or what I was ready for. So I basically kept my mouth closed about being pregnant until I was about 6 to 7 months and just couldn't hide it any more.

Unfortunately by this time the man that I was dating had been caught up by life. Okay okay I guess you can say he was caught by the system or caught by cops. Call it what you want. The streets had enough and he now was incarcerated. I thought that I would be there for him and support him as much as I could. Hell I was carrying his child and as far I was concerned I was in a relationship and in love.

Bubble busted and reality checked at the gate. Went to go visit him belly and all; didn't I get the surprise of my life? Wobbled my young 15 year old pregnant ass up to the jail to visit him and he had the nerve to deny my visit. What? You can't be serious? I'm carrying your child and you're treating me like I'm nothing. I was pissed and confused. I couldn't understand my life. What had I done wrong to deserve this?

What I later found out was he already had a child and he had a child on the way. He later told me that he couldn't accept my visits because than he could not see his other children. So what the hell was I and my child to do? Were we chopped liver? Scraps? Did we mean nothing to him? This made no sense to me at all. I was alone in this with no one and nowhere to turn to. It was becoming my reality at that moment that I had become a statistic.

I battled the feelings of being alone and pregnant. I still attended school for the most part. Once it was no longer concealable, I was offered a chance to attend an alternative school ran by B.O.C.E.S. The program was called the TAP Program. I loved it there.

In this program I was learning things that due to my circumstances I couldn't learn at home. You see, TAP, which stood for TeenAge Pregnancy Program was a program within an educational setting that educated students that were either pregnant or had young children who were still in high school. This program was amazing. It taught me life skills, it prepared me for caring for my newborn, it aided me with an education that was just as challenging as it would've been in a traditional high school. I made friends and networked with other parents where we would get together and do things outside of school with our babies.

TAP gave me the opportunity to make sense of my life and situation. I was proud of myself at that time and in that moment with what I was doing. However, I still had the desire to be with somebody and not have to do this alone. I felt as though the things that I had acquired at school and through experience put me in a very good place for a family.

Yes, I know I was only 15 in age however with the hand that life had dealt me I was only trying to play my cards. So with my daughter's father in jail and me being out in the world single, I decided I wanted to change that. What do you think I did? You guessed it - or maybe you didn't - I found another man.

Hold on though it wasn't just any man it was a man that I met in jail. Yup couldn't get any more street to me than that. It didn't even really matter what he was there for as long as it wasn't rape, murder, abductions or anything with kids. Anything else was just about ok. Don't get me wrong it's not that I condone crime I just felt drugs wasn't such a bad thing when you always see them in the streets.

Anyway, this guy had features that made him quite attractive to me. I was being very superficial at that point in my life. Just wanted to be loved and cared for by someone that respected me and accepted my situation. I wanted someone that didn't want to change me or disrespect me; that was my goal and my thought process. However that didn't become my reality.

Instead what I ran into, was this approximately 6 foot, well built, hazel green eyed man with sandy brown blonde hair with a patch of blonde that wore a killer smile. I say ran into because yes at that time he was my choice, I just know I should've chosen better. Please know that things aren't always as sweet as they seem. Always remember that a lemon is still sour once you brush off the sugar.

When I met him it was toward the end of my pregnancy. I felt as though I had found my knight and shining armor. Once again young and feeling like nobody could tell me a damn thing I was in love - again. He got out of jail and we were damn near inseparable. Before you know it he moved in.

5

Shortly thereafter I gave birth to my first daughter. He was there in the delivery room and he even cut the cord. I finally felt that someone was going to be there for me and that he was going to be good to me. We were going to be a family and raise this little girl together. Things felt good.

We had been together for only a few months before I found out that I was pregnant again. Yes, now 16 years old and baby number two was on the way. To avoid going through the reactions I encountered the first time around I told no one except the father. I figured I was already doing so much on the responsibility level that no one could tell me the wiser. I was young, in love and I wanted to have my children to love and protect them for life. At that time I found it so cute and felt like yeeeeessssss I have a man that loves me and never wants to leave my side. I felt on top of the world, until reality knocked me off.

During this pregnancy things began to change and sour very quickly. He became very controlling. Always yelling, slapping me around, punching me, kicking me, snatching me up by hair the works. What the fuck did I do? Breathe? Wake Up? Fart in my sleep? What? I just didn't know what to do or think. Perhaps this was a phase? Maybe he was stressed due to another baby so soon? I think the glass of water I gave him had too much ice? Oh no or it might have been that the shower I ran for him was too wet? Whatever the reason I was shocked and confused. Then suddenly I felt stuck as if there was no escaping this relationship that turned into a situationship.

I found myself in an abusive relationship for a couple of years. From physical, emotional, sexual, spiritual and mental – if it was abuse I endured it. He tried to end my life on a couple of occasions. He cheated with a close friend and family members. He broke me down, he broke my spirit and he broke my trust in people. When that happens to a person it can be so hard to rebuild.

So I had my second daughter. Now I am the mother of two beautiful baby girls. They are merely 11 months apart. I feel amazing about this. They will grow up together and be the best of friends since they were so close in age was my thought. I was pouring all of my love into them as I silently mourned the loss of my son and hid the abuse that was going on daily.

See when I was about 6 months pregnant, I woke up in a pool of blood. I rushed to the bathroom to clean myself up and to call the doctor to go into her office. I sat on the toilet and a sack splashed into the water below. I cried and cried and cried. I was on the telephone with the doctor and they told me to come right in and bring the sack with me.

I got there and they began all this blood and urine work on me. Checking levels of this and that, I had no clue what they were looking for I just wanted my baby. It seemed to me to be taking forever for them to tell me that I had miscarried. They finally come in the room and they tell me they would like to do a sonogram to be sure that the uterus is clear and okay.

They perform the sonogram and everyone is surprised. The nurse and the doctors both tell me that I was pregnant with twins. My body had what they called a spontaneous abortion and I had lost one of them. However, I was still pregnant with a healthy baby that they would watch me carefully to term. I was confused, emotional, happy, and sad. I didn't know what to feel or think. What I did know was that I had to take it easy for my baby's sake.

I recall times of knives being held to my throat, being choked till I passed out and losing my voice for days, sprained wrists, being punched so hard that I temporarily lost my hearing, being driven in a car all crazy, fast and erratic because he was angry or drinking, fights in front of family members, forced sexual sessions as well as so many other acts of violence towards me. Forced to be away from my family, sleeping in cars and sometimes places where I knew no one or where I was at.

There was so much going on at this point in my life I had no direction. I felt as though I was going around aimlessly doing things just because it was what I did. Not realizing all the other ample opportunities that I could've been taking. I felt that I was a product of my environment and that I was destined to be in this low capacity of living forever.

I remained in this relationship in fear of my life. I was afraid he was really going to kill me one day. So I stayed. Yes, I know that statement is going to be read over and over and over and over and over again. With what I think will read as such the "what the HELL" kind of question in your mind. This is all that I can possibly say to give you a little clarity. With the episodes of issues that were plaguing me, I had little to no concern for my value of life. When you are beaten into the ground verbally and physically you lose some of yourself or all of yourself. I didn't care about myself any longer. Nothing mattered to me except my children.

You are actually afraid to leave. You feel as though if you stay it will stop at least that's the thought. You pray that it'll "never" happen again. Some are victorious enough to survive others have been bought to their demise. Domestic Violence we need to end the silence. Even with that being said I did have my flip switch and he eventually flipped it.

When he threatened to harm my children he didn't realize he was finally flipping the switch. I fought back like no one's business and he had to go. Because for all the threats and promises he had made on my life there was no way in Hell or on God's green Earth that that was going to happen to my babies. Seeing me fight back he only got part of the message so I didn't feel safe staying where I was so I moved.

That started my habit of moving. However moving or trying to run from your problems can sometime only invite the problems to your new found space. So try to deal with things in the space they are manifested in so that you can leave them there when it's time to move on.

Also during that abusive time I was made to drop out of high school. Having two little girls to look up to me I knew that was not the right thing to be doing. So I took my no good English using self-back to school. I reregistered myself, doubled up by taking 11th and 12th grade classes and was able to graduate on time with my graduating class with my two babies in tow. I believe that's when my light grew a wee bit brighter and hope showed up for a second or two. I began to believe in me and I gained a little more hope.

6

I was now a single mother of two, fresh out of an abusive relationship, my mother had just been released from prison with the next major blow in my life. She had served 3 years in a state women's facility. I survived that part felt there could be nothing more tragic.

I was able to live with my wonderful friend Careen from school and her family for a little while. This time was so difficult; I was devastated having my mother incarcerated. I continued to run to the wrong ones in the streets any chance I got. My decision making didn't get any better. I was feeling so damaged and as far as I knew at that time in my life there was no coming back from life's tragedies.

A family meeting was called it was time for the heartbreaking news to be delivered. I recall us sitting around in the room and she had this serious sad look on her face. My mother told us she wasn't well and was going to die. I wasn't trying to hear it; let alone believe it. I lived in my own world of denial. I didn't believe what we had just been told. I had just gone through so much already without my mother and now she's telling me I am going to lose her forever. I truly could not comprehend.

I was overwhelmed with the hand life wanted me to play. I felt as though I needed space. I had already had the practice and experience of holding down the household. Ranging from paying the bills, buying and preparing groceries, cleaning etc etc with a siblings in the house, a nephew and two babies of my own; I had this thing down packed. So I was ready to do this on my own. I had two children I needed to care for and raise. Things were getting too out of hand and I believed it was best to move on to the next chapter in my life.

My next move was my best move and I moved out on my own at the age of 16-17 with 2 children under the age of 4. Once he threatened the safety and lives of my children I had to get out of there. This toxic situation needed to come to an end. I knew that I had to go. It was going to either be him or me; one in the casket and or one in a cell. So I needed to save my children and myself the best way I knew how, I started the game of running.

Besides that, living at home was becoming too much to deal with. I wasn't getting along with my sibling. I wanted to raise my daughters and do the best that I could so I made the executive decision to leave. Life just wasn't being fair.

I moved around like a person in the service or a traveling salesman. I lived more places than I remember at times. Deep down I knew that there had to be something much better than that. This could not be what my life was supposed to be.

Time passed on and I am living on my own with my daughters. Life finally feels livable. I got a job. I began dating just not bringing anyone home. Simple dates; going out to eat, catching a movie, going to bar or lounge. I began to try to get to know people and become a part of society. However it seemed that no matter how hard I tried to stay on the right path life just kept on screwing me.

7

It's now 1995 and I'm about 19 or 20, life decides it has given me as much of a break as it was going to give me at the moment. My nana, my mother's mother, was my best friend. Oh how I loved her so. I could go to her and talk to her about anything and everything. We did so many things together. We would cook and eat, go shopping, go to bingo, she taught me how to sew and I think crotchet or perhaps it was knit, we'd go to church together (as if I had a choice). No matter what we were doing I loved my nana so much!

Don't get me wrong my nana could be very stern when she needed to be. I remember growing up and the things we did. I remember when I thought I was ready to be grown and smoke cigarettes. My nana found out and I just knew I was about to get my own switch off the willow tree that was in her front yard. I swear she probably bought that house because of that tree.

However, no, what a surprise I got from my nana instead. That getting my own switch off of the willow tree wasn't the outcome at all. I actually learned two lifelong valuable lessons. One: my nana told me that if I was ever going to pick up or have a habit make sure that I can afford it. And two: I learned that everything in life if it is done in moderation can be enjoyable if you like it. I learned that because my nana was nice enough to buy me a pack of my favorite brand of cigarettes. Then she made me smoke every last one of them back to back to back. That's right all 20 of them. I thought I was going to die! They tasted horrible.

Yet I learned what I needed to learn from my nana that day. I learned a lesson for life. What's the old saying: "Give a man a fish and he'll eat for a day and if you teach a man to fish he will eat for a lifetime..." It was that type of lesson, I love my nana for that and I live by it.

I laugh now as I think back on all my wonderful memories and life lessons with my nana. My nana was my rock. I enjoyed our Saturday mornings together and meeting up with her at church on Sunday mornings. When we would go to her house on the holidays for big family dinners and barbeques those times were the absolute best. I loved how on Christmas we'd go to her house in the wee hours of the mornings. We went to open gifts and we could already smell the delicious aromas from the kitchen. She'd been up all night preparing Christmas dinner and still happy as a jay bird to see us 4 or 5 am. Those were the days. Those are the memories and traditions I attempt to keep going and create.

Somehow it just doesn't seem to work out when you are the only one that shows up or that tries. I will forever keep trying to keep family together. My family may not understand my actions just know this is and has always been my motive. People only truly die when you allow their memories to fade. My departed loved ones will live on forever.

I know that many of my moves and actions in life have not been understood or perceived in the manner I intended. I get that. I apologize for my past discretions and any and all wrong doing. If I hurt you in the past by anything I've said or done I apologize. I could, at that time, only do what I knew. I am learning how to be better. I cannot turn back the hands of time yet I can and will walk forward in life with a more positive attitude and outlook on things. I know that my attitude determines my altitude and I'm soaring high.

8

It was the beginning of January 1996. My life began to spiral out of control again. I lost my best friend, my nana. She died while in a diabetic coma at the young age of 63. I lost of part of me when she died.

I remember that time so vividly. She had gotten very ill and ended up in a coma due to her diabetes. This had happened around the holidays; you know Thanksgiving and Christmas time. It made the holidays of 1995 so dreary and hard to deal with for everyone. I missed seeing my nana in the kitchen cooking holiday meals and sitting in her infamous seat on the end of the couch to hand out the presents on Christmas morning.

I needed to see her. At first we as the "children had been told not to go to hospital to visit. I'm not sure why I just know I didn't like it. So I would call my aunt to check on my nana all the time.

One particular day I inquired on my nana's condition and I was told she was doing better. I was so happy and overjoyed. I just knew that I needed to see her and hug her and love her. There was so much that I needed to catch her up with.

I went to the hospital and I was traumatized to say the least. My nana was still in a coma. When I entered the area she was in I walked right past her in the bed. The tubes and tape that was covering her face, holding the life support machine attachments in place made it hard for me to recognize her. The beeps and bells from all the alarms and alerts were causing my focus to be feeble.

My nana had the most beautiful freckles, a mole on her nose, bright inviting smile and healthy long nails. I always said I wanted to be like my nana when I grew up. I also wanted nails like that (guess what: now I do). However, do to the involuntary actions her body would make, the medical staff said that they needed to cut them for safety reasons. I was pissed and I was shattered. I just wanted her to get up. To open her eyes, smile at me and let me know that it would all be okay. That moment never took place.

I called my aunt and I was torn apart. I recall hearing the nurses in the room just doing their job. Yet in my mind what I heard was them speaking to my nana as though she was about to respond. My life was never the same. I felt lied to and I was hurt with disappointment. My nana needed me, she needed something and there was nothing I could do to help her. She had always been there for me I wanted to be there for her.

At the time this happened my mother was in the hospital. The family got together and we all went to go visit my mom. It was scene that I never thought I'd be a part of. We all stood around my mother's hospital bed not saying much. We all just look at my mother and at each other in this awkward silence. It was myself, my siblings and my aunts from what I remember.

When no one seemed to be able to come up with the words to tell my mother the news of my nana's passing. I was nudged then told to go ahead and let her know. My heart hit my pinky toe. A lump the size of a model globe formed in my chest and my throat. I do not know how yet somehow I mustered up the words. We all cried and life went kind of black for me since that moment.

Three weeks later my mother passed away at the age of 40. I was devastated, lost and felt so alone and hopeless. Despite what I was going through, I was asked to write both obituaries; I was only 19 or so. I wrote them and even had to read my mother's. I recall being corrected by the pastor because I forgot to mention that she sang in the church or something like that; some things just stand out.

I recall a family dispute with regard to getting the headstone for my mother's grave site. It was very important to me to because to me that symbolized a hat. My mother and I shared something special and that was our love for fashion and style. My mother loved hats. Every chance I got I would surprise her with a hat. Mother's Day, Easter, birthdays etc. sometimes I would buy her a hat just because. She loved hats with detail and character and some had big brims. So when she passed away, it was important to me that she have her final hat. Some family members sang that great old hymn: Sure I can help as soon as I get my income tax.

That song was sung just as the star spangled banner is sung at every game. Yet when the checks came the singing stopped and no one was around to help. So I made it my business to keep my vow to myself and the memory of my mother to get her headstone. Even if I needed to do this alone it was going to get done and it was going to get done now. Yes having the stone in place was a bit of a heart heavy experience. It put things in a true perspective that my mother was gone. It truly made things final and I fell into a deep depression.

I ate at times when I was angry. I ate at times when I was sad. I ate at times when I thought I needed to celebrate that I was out of my "funk" if even for a moment. Either way I ate. I ate everything and anything. I just ate foods that felt good and tasted even better to me at those times.

I had to take custody of my younger sibling when my mother passed away. I did the best I could for several months until that became too much of a task. You know it's hard to raise someone that looks at you and sees their mother yet knows that she's gone. With them knowing I'm just their sister and not that authority figure that should be there.

Attempting to raise someone that thinks they are already grown because nature has given them size before mental growth to match was challenging. My sibling was merely a young teenager and had a growth spirt where he looked like a grown man. He was very tall, broad as well as a bit on the stocky side. So who was I to tell him what to do? Why should he even entertain listening to me? I was only his sister.

So after some major meltdowns and blow out fights another member of the family stepped up and offered for him to stay with her. Meanwhile I continued to try to keep my nose above water still a single teenage parent without a real role model or person to go to for advice or support. I felt so alone and as though I was going from few options to no options.

9

I started dating bad boys and found myself involved with drugs, guns, gangs and other things that I know I didn't sign up for. Yet since I knew the streets I retreated to what was a bit on the familiar side for me. I thought I could be like everybody else in my neighborhood and surroundings and get my hustle on. So I began to sell drugs. I sold different types depending on what was available for me to "re-up" on. Pills, weed, coke and crack cocaine were primarily my choices. I did what I had to do to keep food in my children's mouths, clothes on their backs and a roof over their heads. I took chances daily. I was constantly looking over my shoulder. This was just as bad as being in an abusive relationship with a bully. It didn't feel good looking over my shoulders or feeling paranoid. I was getting tired. I could live this style of life however I wasn't really about that life. I was just trying to look like I was keeping my nose clean and walking the straight and narrow as I continued to do my dirt.

Furthermore, there were other signals that told me I wasn't truly about that life. An incident happened that told me I had a heart and this lifestyle wasn't really for me. You see most people look at the mighty dollar and allow that to consume their thought process and decisions. I couldn't when someone I really cared for and respected came to me begging for drugs and really offering outlandish things. I saw them and this drug game in a totally different light.

I needed to do better if I expected different and better results in my life. So I realized I needed to get out of this drug and street game. Because I not only didn't want to be a part of it, I didn't want the ones I cared for to have it anymore nor did this occupation fit me. I didn't return the product to supplier nor did I sell it to another dealer; I flushed it. Every last gram, pill and bud down the toilet. Everything flushed down the toilet with no second thought and no hesitation.

Did I think there'd be consequences for not having the money or the product? Abso-damn-lutely! Yet, at that time that was nowhere near my thought process. I just wanted and needed to save people that were dying and I felt I needed to stop helping them commit suicide. I needed to do better. This wasn't me and it was so wrong. I felt that I had a responsibility and I could only be accountable for the part that I played.

I needed to at this point not just to change my life however I also needed to change my address - again. I now had someone looking to either get their money for the drugs or they were threatening to kill me. I let them know I didn't have that type of money nor would I. Then I bounced. I took my kids and I moved some more; again and again and again. Running was something I was becoming an expert at.

I needed to do better for my girls and myself so I got out of that and moved; again literally. This time I left New York and moved to the south. That in itself was such a change and drastic move. I went for a visit for a few days, came back to NY gave my civil service/union job my 2 weeks' notice and I left. I left on a Greyhound bus with as much as I could take. Packed up my life in plastic bags and suitcases, grab my girls and then I was gone.

When I first got there I stayed with some friends and then shortly thereafter I found my own place to rent across the street. Being new to the state and the area I felt it would work out better to stay in an area where I knew at least one person. It was a little tough making such a move with no plan in place. Plan A, B, C and money saved. Nope that wasn't me. I was literally winging it and I was stressed the hell out in the process. So what did I do? Yup you got it - I ate.

Things weren't working out the way I had hoped. So after giving it a shot for just under a year I decided it was time to move again. I was attempting to return to New York. Where I hoped to give my children a better life in an area I was familiar with. With a system I could navigate through because I know I was going to need help. I just didn't know how much help I was going to need.

10

*Upon driving back to New York on the 4*th *of July 1999, the radiator on my good ole reliable mode of transportation blew and we were stranded on I-95 for hours in 107 degree weather. The water jugs that were once frozen solid were now melted and the bottles were beginning to get sucked in because it was so hot. The bologna and cheese sandwiches were melted as if they were in a microwave, the peanut butter and jelly sandwiches looked like they were oily juices soaking through bread and as I looked out onto I-95 the road seemed to be moving like waves on the shore. The heat waves danced across the tar as if it was trying to woo it back into a liquid state.*

A few cars stopped to try to help us. One older couple stopped and allowed me to use their cell phone. Another couple stopped and offered me a few dollars and I used their phone as well. Then finally as the night was just about to set in one guardian angel by the name of Jacqueline Bolden saved us. She offered for us to sit in her air conditioned car with her and her nephew. She was going from Virginia to DC to take her young nephew to see fireworks.

Jacqueline let me use her phone yet I was still unable to reach anyone. I couldn't get anyone in New York to answer nor could I reach anyone from where I was coming from. I felt my soul drowning as my insides welled up with tears. The lump in my chest had risen to the top of my throat and I felt as though I was going to erupt. I felt that every turn I took was right smack into a dead ended brick wall. I had to keep it together so that the girls didn't get upset or panic. So I held all my tears and emotions back as Jackie and I sat just off the I-95 at a rest stop trying to devise a plan. Since it was the fourth of July Jackie had some sparklers with her and her nephew. They shared them with the girls. I watched them running around happily as if there wasn't a worry in the world.

Jackie was in the process of moving, so she just so happened to have two apartments. Jackie had the apartment she was presently living in and also her new apartment that she had already signed her new lease for. She offered me and my daughters a place to stay. I was hesitant at first yet what options at this hour of night with no money, no phone, no food, no plan, no transportation did I really have.

We stayed with her for a few weeks. We lived in her new apartment until it was time for her to move in. Daily she would take me out to see Richmond, Virginia. She would take me out to see the potential of living there if I in fact decided to remain in Virginia. Jacqueline was such a blessing. She did things for me and my girls that I thought were unheard of. Some of the simplest things that threw me for a loop were the facts that she cared and never knew me from a whole in the wall before she stopped on I-95.

Jackie didn't know me from a can of paint and here she was helping me when I couldn't get anyone else to extend a hand. When I had finally reached a few family and friends they basically in a nutshell couldn't, wouldn't just or didn't help. Jackie also was working for Philip Morris at the time and offered to help me get a job if I was interested. I felt so overwhelmed with gratitude, however at the same time I was struggling with the desire to get back up North to New York.

I know that I took the chance to move to the South because I felt it was more affordable and I'd do better. That really didn't work because I did it without a real plan. Nothing saved up and nothing laid out. That may work for some however it most definitely didn't work for me that time.

So after a few weeks she helped me get on an Amtrak train to get back to New York. I had to leave everything behind except two small suitcases, the clothes on our backs, food to travel and 50.00 in my pocket for myself and my children to start over with. The journey was without a doubt a rollercoaster ride however I was ready for so much more at this point in my life.

Jackie had renewed my faith in people, in good things happening and having a little patience. I am ever so grateful for Jackie and all that she did for me and my daughters. I am ever so appreciative of the impression she left in my life.

We don't seem to look at your strengths until strength is all we have. Believe in yourself and be kind to yourself. You deserve as much as you give to anyone or anything else. Certain time is allowed to us to get to know ourselves. Why does there have to be a limit though? We just need to take that time to do the same for ourselves as we'd take for anything or anyone else that we find important and worthwhile.

We need to get to know our strengths and weaknesses. Be open and honest with yourself. Why lie to yourself when you already know the truth? We just need to not be so afraid. You've already made it this far you're a survivor! You're strong and you can make it. Look at it this way if you're reading this book: CONGRATULATIONS!!

I want to be the first to congratulate you on your 100% success rate of making it through life's ups and downs! You're stronger than you give yourself credit for. Don't quit now. We tend to try to run from our situations and circumstances not realizing that we cannot run from ourselves. Remember if you don't take care of yourself you cannot continue to care for anyone else.

11

My children and I, got back to New York with the expectation of being able to stay with family, temporarily, yet that didn't happen. The family that I reached out to told me there was no room at the inn. They had me feel like I was outside of the manger on Christmas Eve. I was told: I have room for the girls just not everybody; translation I can help the kids just not you. Then there were others that just flat out said no.

It was something that I just couldn't understand. I thought back on how many times family and friends had always somehow ended up living with me. They lived with me with their kids, without kids, moved in mates, treated mi casa like su casa and guess what they did this rent free. That wasn't the agreement, it was just how it turned out. I cooked all the meals and paid all the bills yet I couldn't get a help up even though I helped everyone out. Now wasn't that about a bitch. Well you live and you learn. And in my case I had to learn fast.

I had to make due and face the fact that I was now going to have to be creative. I would find friends that had children around the same age as my girls and they would stay over nights. I would return every morning to get them asking how the party was. I made so these "slumber parties" were fun for the girls since the reality was life was about to get really different and very difficult.

We were officially homeless. The girls would be safe and sound for the night with friends or a family member. I rode the subways and buses from first stop to last stop, trying to think of plans for the next 24 hours. Basically I called myself just buying time. I slept in parks, benches in terminals, abandoned buildings and sometimes vacant houses when I could.

At times I would find myself in situationships just trying to make it through a 24 hour period. Yet I needed to buy a little more time as I tried to figure out this part of my life. Being in places, with people and things that I could never imagine had to come to an end. I needed stability and I needed guidance.

Contemplating my options and at times feeling as though I had none. I was learning and experiencing that life could get darker than I ever imagined. Seeing sides of this thing called life that people only read about in books or would see in the movies. The streets were no place for a family, for an individual. The streets were no place I wanted my children to recall as home.

After doing this for a couple of months, I was blessed to stay with some friends in the Bronx. I knew nothing about living in the city being from the suburbs on Long Island. However I was getting a crash course and I had to learn on the fly. That meant learning the streets and avenues, subways and buses, connections and closures. I swear that felt like I was learning a foreign language being in the boroughs of New York. I'd never done so much traveling just trying to get from point A to point B .

The wonderful friends that stepped up to help me were TJ and Rhonda. TJ introduced me to his wife and family. My children and I felt so welcomed in their home. They made us feel right at home. I had met TJ when I was a party promoter and event coordinator. He knew little about me yet he knew my work ethic and I'm glad that spoke for something.

It's not always about the money you have. It can be about your skills, your resources or anything you feel you have that has value. Learn to barter again. Never feel that because you do not have a dollar in your pocket that you aren't with resources. You are your greatest source or resources. You are valuable. You have to see and believe in your value, potential and worth before you can pass it off to anyone else.

Rhonda was a godsend! Having children and a family of her own she was able to show me how to balance work, home and play. I was always feeling overwhelmed and lost about my situation. I didn't seem to know my ass from my elbow at times. I felt as though I wasn't going to make it, like I was the ultimate failure and like my rock bottom had no bottom. I felt like I was steadily falling at an unbelievable rate with nothing to stop my momentum.

Due to the way things seemed to line up in my life I became an all about business type. Very regimented, structured, by the book; I felt as though I couldn't waiver off track. I believed that there was only one way for things to go right since the other ways things always seemed to go wrong.

I had to learn to learn. I had to learn that life is like a maze. Life is A-Maze-ing! It is so amazing because there are always options. The options only end when you stop trying. Rhonda and I would sit up and talk for hours. Rhonda said so many things that stuck with me and she showed how to manage so many parts of my life that I felt were unmanageable. I had finally found balance or at least a sense of it. Rhonda had 6 children at the time that I met her; ranging from infant to teenager. She showed me how to do things that could entertain the children as well as me to pass the time. She showed me how to love, show love and accept love. She taught me how to take time for myself and have time for my children and not feel guilty about it. Rhonda taught me how to live and be okay about it.

Through this struggling process and this battle with myself, Rhonda helped me find direction and a bit of purpose. My hope was being restored and my faith was beginning to grow in strength and abundance. I felt as though I was neither a failure at being a mother nor a failure at existing as an individual. I was learning that I had just made some choices that either were poor judgement or that I had not considered all the possible results before moving forward.

Life is all about balance. It was unknown to me how to balance out what I was dealing with and what I needed to do. Always feeling stressed and overwhelmed, Rhonda and I would have heartfelt honest talks after all the little people were settled down for the night. Having a friend that not only had great advice yet also had the talent to just listen is a priceless thing to have.

Rhonda helped to instill so much in me that I may not have learned from anyone else. Things that I needed to learn in my life at that time. Timing is everything. Learning about this balance assisted me with making it through this part of my life.

It was coming close to September which would be when the children would need to start school. I felt as though I could no longer stay with Rhonda and her children. I knew it was time to move on. During the summer it was fun and games for the children to have "sleepovers" and sleep on the floor. However with them needing to go to school they needed a good night's sleep in their beds. So I thanked Rhonda for everything and me and my children left with my two small suitcases filled with all we had.

I left Rhonda's and stayed with another friend in the Bronx. However the space there was tight and I couldn't see myself living on someone's living room floor for long. I didn't want to crowd their space or wear out my welcome. I needed a new plan; a plan that could be a true game changer for the status of me and my children. I needed a plan that was a step toward longevity and permanency. I had begun to acquire hope and faith and now I needed to put things into action to see results.

12

After staying with different friends in the five boroughs and Nassau County, I decided that the next best step was to go into the shelter in the city. I couldn't expect to sleep on couches and floors forever. I had to end staying in places where you could watch rats and mice run marathons with no fear of anyone or anything in the clear break of day.

I needed a home for me and my children. Going through the system I knew would be challenging. I was up for the challenge. I had already gotten through so many others. However I was unaware of how challenging it was going to be to even get into the shelter system. I actually went there about four times before they deemed me "homeless" to their definition and standards. Not giving up, they finally wanted to offer me help.

See according to the system I was not homeless as long as I had "a place" to stay regardless of the conditions or circumstances. I explained to them the first time that I went there that I had just come back to NY from another state and I had nowhere to go. I had to prove my trip to them and I needed to prove when I arrived. They saw that I had arrived longer than 14 days prior so they said I had to have had a place to stay for the past 2 weeks. They denied me help and said I wasn't homeless.

The next day I decided to return to the homeless intake office. Once again with my daughters and my two small suitcases in tow, I was there because I needed help. I was determined not to take no for an answer. This time I told them that I was staying with a friend and sleeping on the floor with my children. The procedure was that they needed to interview the head of household and even though they were told there was no space for permanent or temporary residency for me and my children the system once again told me; you're not homeless.

I couldn't give up. I had dreams and visions for myself and my girls and they didn't have the streets as my home. I had to keep trying. I knew the facts of my situation and I wasn't going to have a system tell me any different. I had to be consistent and persistent. I returned again telling them that I was temporarily staying with someone that has a large family and not enough space for me and my family. Once again the system denied me. I finally appealed one last time and had to truly fight my case. I had to attend a small hearing and everything.

Being persistent and consistent; I did it. I was finally eligible to be considered "homeless" by the system. What a thing to want to celebrate! Yup I was celebrating that I was no longer unofficially homeless however I was now officially categorized as homeless. Go figure, the things I would find to eat about. Some people would run to drugs, cigarettes or the liquor bottle. I ran to food. Food was my drug of choice.

I went through the system in about a year and a half to two years. It wasn't the best experience however it wasn't the worst. There are many hidden treasures in life's situations sometimes you just have to pay attention. They may not even reveal themselves to you right away. Just know that I now overstand that everything in life definitely happens for a reason. The struggles you are going through today are preparing you for the steps you may need to take tomorrow.

After going through about 5 different shelter locations throughout the process of being homeless, throughout all 5 boroughs except for Staten Island, I received my keys to my apartment in Queens, NY. I was ecstatic and oh so blessed. I knew this was where'd I would be for the long haul. This apartment was going to be home from this day forward. No more shelters. No more signing in and out, no more house meetings regarding rules and regulations, no more inspections, no more weekend authorization passes, etc. etc. etc. I was finally on my way to gaining my independence back. I had my footing for my foundation finally laid.

13

I lived in this amazing 7 story apartment that had the most spectacular view of the NYC skyline. I use to love to sit with my children and watch the fireworks from our window that where going on in the city on the Hudson or the East River. We'd watch the beautiful sunsets and the vibrant color patterns that would illuminate the top of the Empire State Building. This apartment gave us such joy. It was really starting to feel like home until a few major events happened that made me feel uneasy and uncertain of life and its future.

First of all I met a man. We dated. That all sounds wonderful right? Wrong. This man brought situations and things into my life that I most definitely didn't condone. I was disappointed and utterly crushed. I had put so much hope into this. However when you start to bring things into my circle unsolicited and unwanted you and you habits need to go. Meanwhile, as I cried I ate. Didn't want to be bothered by nothing and no one.

Because of what I was going through in this failing relationship that was clearly more of a situationship I turned to a friend for comfort, support and understanding. Let's say he was very supportive and encouraging. So much support that I found out a few months later I was going to have a baby. I was inundated with everything that was going on in my life. Now here I was again repeating history. A single mother trying to find her way and survive on her own for her and her children; that seemed to be the story of my life.

I had already been through so much and made it, I had to keep pushing. Being broke and doing a lot of running around I was losing weight so in my mind it was okay to now eat what I wanted when I wanted just because I was pregnant. Being stressed about doing this, single parenting, all over again after 10 years made me feel so deluged. I was so foggy even on the most clearest of days so what did I do - I ate.

During this time I was going through issues as an individual, my children were also beginning to grow and deal with situations of their own. They were very active. I kept them in activities like sports and dance, they just began having issues with friends, issues in school, puberty etc. etc. etc. When you are a single parent there is no time out for you when your children need you. Your issues are just not that pertinent when your children have their own things going on. Each child is an individual and individually they were dealing with their own things. I was overwhelmed all over again. I was exhausted with worries and stressors that I had no idea how to deal with. For the sake of my pregnancy and mental health I knew I needed to get a hold on things and soon.

Then just a week after I gave birth to my third bundle of joy; 9/11 happened. From the 7th story apartment window I could see more than I wanted to visualize. 9/11 is a day that is forever etched in the hearts and minds of many in the world. It happened literally in my own backyard. It was a sight I can never erase.

Here I am home just getting back to sleep from bringing my two older ones to school that day. I had dozed off for a bit to be awakened by a phone call. I recall the caller asking me how the kids and I were and if everything was okay. I said yes still half asleep. I may not have been fully alert yet I recall without question the stillness and eeriness that was stifling the room. There was such a deafening heavy silence in the air.

They began to talk about the acts of terror that had just happened with the first tower in the heart of Manhattan. I quickly jumped up and ran to my Livingroom window. I saw nothing except clouds of thick black smoke spewing across the New York sky. Just as I went to return to the phone a quick flash of orange, red, yellow and what looked like blue flames with clouds of smoke ranging in all hues of white, grey and black filled my sights. I hung up the phone, grabbed my week old newborn daughter, my slippers and my keys and ran a block and a half in my pajamas to pick up my children from school.

I was so terrified. I felt that if life was going to end we'd do it together. I know how I felt when I was left alone when my mother and my nana passed away. I didn't want them to suffer like that at all. Yes, I may have been thinking a bit on the selfish side at that moment however that was all that was on my mind. I loved my children and I just knew they needed to be home with me as safe as we could be.

We either all made it together or we would all go together. My heart will always go out to families that lost loved ones that day. I still have flashes of those sights. It was so devastating that I couldn't eat. This time I couldn't keep anything down and that to me became the solution to losing weight.

14

The next year was rockier than the last. I found out that I was pregnant again. I was happy and nervous all at the same time. Doing this single parenting thing over and over again alone was becoming a vicious cycle. Nonetheless I was ready for the challenge. This time I was pregnant by an old flame that I tried to rekindle life with. As I've been known to say I'll say it again: Sometimes you gotta let it go...

I was just unaware and unprepared for the challenges I was about to face. So there was this particular afternoon and I was 22 weeks pregnant. I was feeling very energetic and had the taste for seafood. I was spending the day with my girls and my great friend Mimi who actually became a housemate. Anyway everything was going amazing that day.

We were sitting around watching and singing the songs to one of my all-time favorite movies *The Five Heartbeats*. I recall rushing from the kitchen into the Livingroom to sing one of my favorite parts of the movie. The kids laughed and then joined in. I finished my mini performance and went back into the kitchen to finish my seafood smorgasbord. I was cooking everything: fish, shrimp, scallops, crab cakes and crab legs. I'm blaming it on the pregnancy however I wanted it all so I just had to have it.

After cooking everything and feeding everyone I actually had no appetite. I remember just wanting to lie down and rest. I woke up with the worst pains and cramps in my stomach. I couldn't understand. I thought these can't be contractions. There was no way I could be in labor. I was only 22 weeks pregnant. This couldn't be happening. I called the ambulance to go to the hospital. Mimi stayed at home with the girls.

Once I arrived at the hospital and they examined me, I was found to be already 3 centimeters dilated. I was so scared and my anxiety level was through the roof. I'd given birth alone before just never to a baby that wasn't ready for world according to nature's standards. I was just about 5 months pregnant; I was alone and terrified.

The doctor explained that I needed to be admitted. They placed in a Trans lumbar bed. This bed basically had me damn near upside down. It was necessary for me to be in this position because not only was I already dilating but my baby was breech and attempting to enter the world. It was way too soon. I didn't know what to do. The position of the bed plus gravity was supposed to keep my baby inside. I just cried and prayed it would work and work soon.

Honestly at this point all I could do was pray. Pray for the contractions to stop, pray the pain to go away, pray that the baby would just wait a little while longer to be born. I just laid there in this upside down position crying with tears rolling down the sides of my face and clogging my ears. The nurse came in to console me as the doctor came into reexam me.

Regardless of what hopes and prayers myself and the medical staff had this baby had a plan of its own. The doctor told me I had to deliver I was already 5 to 6 centimeters dilated and with the baby being in a breech position, the baby was beginning to go into distress. I couldn't stop crying and I began hyperventilating. They had to calm me down. My current state was in no means helping me, my baby or my situation.

I was whisked off from the labor and triage area over to the delivery room. The whole way down the hallway, which seemed to me to be never ending with lights whizzing by on the ceiling, all I could do was think why?! . We enter into this cold room where everything seems to happen so fast.

Bells ringing, alarms beeping, the click and clacking of the sterile metal instruments being laid out and prepared to be used. Doctors and nurses talking and everything sounding all muffled due to everyone being in mask as if this was a secret mission. There was so much activity and presence in the room I felt as though they wheeled me into a conference. The doctors and nurses were everywhere.

I was feeling as though I was a spectator in all this. I mean I have already had 3 full term healthy babies why was this happening now like this? Why did this time have to be so tumultuous? What had gone wrong? There seemed to be no real reason at that moment except this was a plan that was out of my hands.

Many pushes and cries later, the doctor announced it's a boy. I cried because I was happy, I had a son to join the family that only consisted of my girls and me. I was overfilled will love and oh so ecstatic. I cried because I was scared and unsure. I cried because I was blessed, excited and abundantly emotional. I just continued to cry. I cried so much my eyes and my throat got dry and soar.

My son, Isaiah Ka'Ron, was born into this world on May 6, 2002. He entered this world on a silent note. That made me very nervous. Why wasn't my son crying? What was wrong? The medical staff hustled and bustled around the room doing all types of things. Finally I heard the faint cry of my little man. He came into this world weighing 1 pound 1 ounce. His feet and hands were smaller than half my thumb. He had hair and eyebrows. His little face was full of so many expressions.

In the split second that I got to see him I absorbed so much. My family was complete with little Isaiah. The girls were so excited to hear about their new little brother. They were however equally confused and sad when I explained that he would need to remain in the hospital and what it meant to be premature. This was so tough. Here I was trying to explain something to my children that I really didn't even understand. I couldn't really convince myself that everything was going to be alright. So I'm not sure how convinced they were about what I was saying to them either.

So Isaiah was transferred from the hospital in Queens to a more suitable hospital in Manhattan that specialized in neonatal care. I was dealing with separation anxiety already and I wanted my son to be with me. The next day when I was discharged, I collected my belongings and traveled via public transportation from Queens to New York City with everything I had with me. I was determined to be with my son as soon as possible by any means necessary.

The next couple of days were really touch and go. Everytime the phone rang my heart would drop and skip a beat or three. I prayed hard for my son's health and strength as well as for my family to be whole and one again. As a unit we were struggling to stay together and be on the same page. This rollercoaster ride was one I had no idea about. I had never fathomed anything that was about to take place.

On May 10, 2002, I was returning home from seeing my son in the hospital and dropping the girls off so I could get a little respite time. I was crossing the street with my dear friend Mimi and a car runs a red light and creams into us. Hitting us and crashing into us like pins on a bowling lane. This couldn't be happening. All I could remember thinking about were my children. Are they going to be okay?

I promise you I can't make this up. So just to recap before I move on from this segment: I had a son prematurely, I was hit by a car a few days later, and I then couldn't travel from Queens to Manhattan on public transportation due to my injuries. I called on a reliable friend by the name of Raheem. Raheem would come to pick me up after he left work at the hair salon. He would drive me to see my son in Manhattan. That was such a godsend. Seriously the time that he gave me with my son was priceless.

Although Isaiah's conditions was critical and very touch and go I was blessed with the opportunity to hold my son for the very first time when he was about 2 weeks old. It was skin to skin. Even though I know his heart rate was faster than mine I still can say that my anxiety caused our hearts to beat as one. I felt as though we were in sync. That moment is one that will never fade.

Just as I am soaking up the moment, all types of alarms start to go off on the baby monitor. The staff came rushing over to me and I froze. I wanted to hand Isaiah to the nurse so she could care for him however they worked on him right there in my arms. They were bagging him and giving him air compressions. His vitals starting dropping while I was holding my son, I was stuck in shock not knowing what to do but cry. I thought he was going to die in my arms. I thought that my stolen moment was causing me to steal his last moments. I was so scared and emotional. I began to feel guilty.

The staff got Isaiah stabilized and placed him back in the incubator. I just sat there with him for hours gently stroking his skin and letting him know that I was forever there by his side. I had been told by staff that the more physical contact and affection a premature baby felt the better his chances could be. So I was determined to give my son all the love, affection and positive energy I could to support him in his fight for life.

Every night and on his days off, Raheem made sure that I got to the hospital to spend the necessary time I needed to spend with my son. There were so many ups and downs, not only throughout this time, yet in the course of the day. Isaiah put up one hell of a fight with his little self. Yet, on the early morning of May 26, 2002, I received that dreaded call. It was the doctor from the hospital; Isaiah had fought his last fight.

My son fought for life for 20 days. Born at 1 pound 1 ounce, Isaiah fought as long as his heart could fight. His eyes were still closed at birth yet we were blessed to see into each other's soul through our eyes for a long heartfelt moment when I held him. I saw my son and my son saw me. These are memories that I will cherish for a lifetime. His brown little chinky eyes sparkled in that moment that we shared. That will forever be our moment; our time and ours alone.

There are so many things that hurt about that time period yet there are also moments that stand out that allow me to smile just a little bit too. Many people do not get the chance that I got. Such as to hold my premature son, for my son to grip my finger making it feel like the tightest grip on Earth and to look into each other's eyes were our souls seemed to connect not only for that moment but for a lifetime.

Yet I am human. I fell into a bout with depression. I was inconsolable at times. I was now making arrangements for my son to be buried with my mother. I had absolutely no money for my son's services. I was blessed to find a funeral home that worked with me and truly made this transition as peaceful as possible. I'd like to once again say Thank you Mr. Kenneth Brewster and staff at Crowes Funeral Home in Jamaica, NY.

At the time when my heart was aching and my soul was bleeding you helped to bandage my wounds so I could make it through. And to Pastor Jerry Turner Thank You for officiating my son's home going service and providing me with words of support and encouragement that I needed. Thank you for the prayer sessions as well. I don't know how I would've made it through without you. Thank you, thank you and thank you.

15

I fell into such a depression at first I wouldn't eat. Then I found myself going through periods where I would sort of hoard food. I'd buy snacks, snacks and more snacks; I made sure that daily my "fat snack pack" was full of all the things I felt I would need throughout the night. I would eat when no one was watching as if that meant that I wasn't eating. I guess what wasn't seen didn't count. I would sometimes eat until I was sick. Literally, throwing up until my stomach felt like it was turned inside out and on fire. I just couldn't regulate my eating habits, my weight or my feelings. I was so lost.

I knew that this wasn't the way to manage my weight or my health so I voluntarily put myself in therapy. Counseling is something that I have learned is there if and when I need it. I had the power and mindset to know when I needed that extra support. I had to get out of my own way, quit blocking my blessings and be positive that this was all possible.

Knowing what I needed I found the right therapist for me. I'll admit not every therapist patient relationship works. I had to find a therapist that was going to understand me and my way of expressing myself. I needed someone that was going to respect my process and guide me through possible alternative methods of dealing with issues. After meeting with a few therapists, I found the perfect match that I needed to help me through this trying period in my life.

Once I began to function a little better and the terror alert was lowered, I felt as though things would be manageable. I had my little minimum wage job; I was handling my business and family situations. I felt like I was back on a plateau or a slow upward climb. It was starting to feel as though life was going to be great for once. Like all the nonsense was gone and I was going to make it out of the pits of hell I'd been living in. Thought I was heading on top of the world. How soon does reality check me again? Trust me it checked me and it checked me hard.

A hot water pipe burst in my kitchen and flooded my entire apartment. The water came erupting out of the wall and knocked the cabinet door off the hinge. Hot steam, rust and scolding hot water began to stream throughout the apartment. We had just gone to bed about an hour or so prior. As the water rushed down the hallway of the apartment I recall asking the girls who left the water running. As I opened my bedroom door which was located at the end of the hallway and I saw all this hot water I yelled to kids to get on their beds and stay off the floor.

I put on several pairs of socks and my heavy work boots and rushed down to the kitchen. I grabbed anything I could and wrapped it around my hand and arm to reach under the sink to turn off the valves. The apartment was totally flooded. Furniture, clothes, computer, paperwork etc. etc. etc. all ruined and floating in the rusted hot water. My life that I had just put together was now all washed away. I was devastated and lost. The tears that flowed down my face seemed to be adding to the flood that was running down the walls from my 7th floor apartment and now ruining the apartments underneath me all the way down to the 4th floor.

My neighbor's property was getting all messed up due to this and I was feeling so responsible. Televisions and electronics, furniture, clothes in closets, carpets, and pictures of family, art work etc. I didn't know what to do. I had no monies to replace my own belongings let alone to replace someone else's things as well. I had to move again and that's when I decided to move back to Long Island.

I filed a claim with management to try to come to a settlement. They accepted my paperwork and pictures then they made me an offer. They offered me $50.00. Yup for all my belongings and my life possessions I was valued at $50.00. I couldn't believe it. I was flabbergasted. I refused their offer and they came back with a second offer of $75.00. I knew at this point I was going to need some assistance.

I reached out to my local congresswoman for assistance because I was at a loss and at my wits end. After many meetings and displaying my evidence she was able to assist me with getting a transfer from Queens out to Long Island. As I stated this had been a part of my plan all along. I had wanted to move back to Long Island because I knew the system, I knew the area and I knew how to obtain the things that I may have needed for myself and my children to make it through. I also wanted to move out of an apartment and into a house. I was looking for space to enjoy and entertain. I needed a space for my children to play and grow for a long time to come.

So I took this opportunity to do just that. I found a house in Long Island that seemed like the perfect fit and the perfect deal. This house had enough rooms and space for everyone. It also had a yard for cookouts and spending family time. Everything looked like it was falling into place.

16

Things aren't always worth the value of its shine. You really have to investigate things, some things more thoroughly than others, and really look below the surface. This truly goes to the old saying that everything that glitters ain't gold.

While all of this is going on, the girls are growing and going through their own individual stages of life and finding themselves. Many times as a parent we are required to put ourselves on hold and our needs on the backburner for our children. Just because we need to take a pause doesn't mean that we don't count.

I lost myself many times on this journey. I lost myself in my children. I lost myself in work. I lost myself in my children's extracurricular activities. I lost myself in friends. I would just continue to lose myself. I'll admit because of what was going on in my life, there were times I may have accidently lost myself on purpose. Sometimes those times just made my life feel a little easier to deal with because it wasn't my life alone. I'm not by any means complaining. I am merely stating that when we lose ourselves in something or someone else we tend to forget about ourselves. That isn't good for anyone. Take care of you just as you take care of everyone else.

One daughter was into being with friends and "doing her". She was always keeping me on my toes; a bit of a rebellious teenager, coming in late, being defiant and running away. My other daughter was into sports, dance and singing. Don't get me wrong she too could have an attitude to boot too. While the baby, she was just being a baby. I tell you my house was considered to me as the House of Hormones. Didn't know many times if I was coming or going yet I do know that I was eating.

Despite all the ruckus and the rigmarole that life was dealing me I still had things to do, people relying on me, deadlines to meet, bills past due and bills overdue etc. etc. etc. There was no break for breathing let alone anything else. However trust and believe I found time to eat. I ate all the wrong things at the wrong times. Yet I felt I had to eat something to "keep up my strength" and to "keep me going".

I was beside myself. No matter where I seemed to turn for help I seemed to run into judgement. All types of negativity. Fingers being pointed, hurtful negative words being thrown around like a lasso at a rodeo with the freedom of the wind I was not going to stand for this. Felt like the world was against me and as if no one really gave a damn if I made it or not. Who are you? Don't judge me...

I seemed to constantly run into people that would say call me if you need anything. Then the minute I needed something either I found no answer when I called or no one had anything at all; not even time for me. I believe people really need to say what they mean and mean what they say. Don't tell me what you think I want to hear because I'm not holding positions for pacifiers. Be real with me is all I ask, I'm a big girl I can handle it. In the words of the late Mrs. Nancy Reagan: Just Say No!! If there's something you really do not want to do or you simply cannot do it: Just Say No.

I go through the process of getting together the broker fee, security and first month rent payments. That was no easy task to obtain yet through grace and dyer persistence it happened. I get all my stuff that I salvaged from the flood, which wasn't much and moved me and my family into this house. I am at that moment overjoyed and feeling oh so blessed. I was feeling as though this was the beginning that I needed to rewrite my story. BAM!! Things in my life once again began to shift my happiness on to a quick stressful unsolicited ride.

Where does one begin not wanting to give you the long version? I have no clue because even the short version may find itself a little lengthy. So like I said I managed to muster all the necessary monies needed to make the move from Queens to Long Island. That would be first month's rent, security and broker's fee, moving truck, boxes and transportation for myself and the kids and a few other miscellaneous expenses. All this was needed to be secured on a minimum wage salary of about $7.50 an hour and a whole lot of faith.

The move was so necessary therefore the expense didn't even matter. You know the saying: You have to rob Peter to pay Paul. Well I was willing to beg and borrow from Peter, to run and hide from Peter and Paul. Yup it was that serious.

I made it happen too. So we moved in and the first few months were going fine until life decides it was time to start "happening" again. Life is always happening it was time to buckle up for the roller coaster ride.

17

In September of 2007, we make the move and up until about March or so of 2008 things went well. On February 29, 2008 I became the proud Glam-Ma to a beautiful baby girl. I was so happy and full of emotions seeing her enter into this world. See it never fails where there is darkness there is light and in the light there too is darkness. I see my life as the ying and the yang; if it were to be a picture. With all this joy, one would think that there were no worries in the world, it was quite the contrary.

The landlord decided that he wanted to do work on the house. That sounds great, right? WRONG!! However the work he was performing was for his benefit. He began to make the home an illegal two family home. Leaving me with faulty heating, many times no heat or hot water, wildlife began to take over the outer perimeters of the house, the attic space and invade areas inside the house as well - raccoons, possums, squirrels and mice. There was one time we caught 17 mice in less than 4 days. Sometimes there were 3 and 4 caught on a trap at a time.

It was getting so bad; the raccoons had begun to tear holes in ceiling. I'd come home to find piles of sheetrock dust and plaster in different areas of the house. One evening I came home to a hole so big in the ceiling I could see the claws of the raccoon trying to come down. I was scared shitless. I notified the landlord and he never responded. I called wildlife trappers and exterminators and either the estimates were too high for me to pay or they stated that since I was only the tenant, the property owner had to contract their services. So I had to get creative to try to fix this myself. I took a thick board, a thick big cardboard box, a cement block and a broom; I wedged them between the ceiling and the floor praying I never saw them move.

Unfortunately on many occasions I felt as though my prayers were going unanswered. I would spend many nights literally staring at the ceiling. Watching for raccoons at night and squirrels in the day. There would be so many squirrels it would sound as if they were moving furniture and having a party in the attic and the wall spaces all day long, especially on cold or rainy days.

On top of all that, the house began to lean. I would come in from work and the dresser drawers would be open, things on the coffee table would be slid forward and sometimes cabinet doors would be slightly ajar. It would look like someone was trying to ransack my house. If that was the case they would only be practicing because I didn't have much. Before I realized why things looked like this, I thought maybe even the animals made it in and back out somehow. I was clueless and slightly paranoid.

Things were so hazardous something had to be done. The town was notified and they came out and did an inspection. They wrote up all the violations and gave the landlord a time frame to complete them. All I could do was hope and pray because my request for repairs went unanswered. Yet there were times I'd come home from being at work all day and work had been done on the illegal portion of the house. I was boiling inside. I had been sectioned off from part of the house. I now had to use the back door to enter my "portion" of the house.

There was no type of security or motion sensor light on the outside of the house. There would be times we would come home to a family of raccoons on the back porch as if we were the ones that dropped by for a visit. I never ever wanted to put the garbage out until the morning it was to be picked up because I didn't want it to be the calling card to wildlife. The house itself already seemed to be a magnet for that without any help. And let's not talk about when I barbequed, the cleanup had to be done right away and thoroughly. Just trying to prepare and enjoy a meal from the grill was becoming a stressful adventure more so than an enjoyable experience.

Things were beyond out of hand. I was so angry and annoyed. I was so occupied and busy throughout the day that at times I'd forget to eat then that night I'd eat and snack like I was going to run a marathon that day. The truth being I was going right to sleep. The pounds just packed on and my health wasn't getting any better. Stressed out, overwhelmed, underpaid, overworked, underappreciated, the list goes on and on and on. My health wasn't even a thought while all this was going on.

Might I add that life never ask for your vote as to when enough is enough. Nope no way no how life just keeps happening and it happens at its own pace. Doing exactly what life wants when life wants. You're just supposed to run alongside of life until you catch up. Newsflash you won't catch up. You can't catch up. Know that every time you stopped trying life kept going. You just need to take a moment to find that point to start from. All you can do really is live in the moment. Be in the now and focus on yourself.

I was so done with my past and my present; I couldn't even see a future. There were times I could not see myself reaching the age of 25, 30 even 40 years of age. Truth be told I never thought I'd be here now at this age in this moment writing this book. Ha Ha #WontHeDoIt!

18

I got the surprise of a lifetime when I was approached by my oldest daughter now about 16 telling me how she didn't feel well. She walked into my bedroom with her stomach exposed rubbing it telling me she felt sick. The first thing that I noticed was the infamous black line of life that runs up the stomach of many pregnant women. I damn near died. Hell, I now felt sick too.

I asked her about her period because I know I had been supplying pads and things of that nature. I even asked about boys and sex which Lord knows this wasn't the first touch on the topic. She told me the same thing she had always told me and that was she wasn't having sex.

Ummmm, well I knew that not to be true. So I made a call to the local clinic and made her an appointment for a pregnancy test. Yup, you guessed it. It was positive and there was nothing else for me to do except go to the store and buy 2 boxes of Newport 100's and start a habit I had quit 3 years prior. She was already 6 months pregnant, there no other options other than to prepare for a new addition to the family. My baby was having a baby.

Did I think she was ready? Absolutely not. If it was up to me this would have had to be a blessing that was put on hold. There were already a tremendous amount of struggles we were dealing with. I could barely get her to go to school or follow through with things without the responsibility of a baby. However it wasn't my plan it was apparently the plan of a higher power and that was completely out of my control.

So as a single mother, who knew this path all too well, I prepared myself and attempted to prepare my daughter for the changes that one could only expect. I knew that there was no manual that could tell her, me or you about every twist and turn, up and down, in and out that life could put you through. Hell that book is still in the process of being researched and lived out today. The possibilities are endless. Yet you cannot always convince someone that feels as though they already know everything. Sometimes you have to get out of the way so folks can move on their path, after barricading the exit for so long. However I'm stubborn as hell so I didn't see myself throwing in the towel or stepping aside as an option.

My daughter didn't stop being defiant just because she was pregnant. Like many teens that go through this, she really believed that now that she was about to have a baby, she was really grown. She didn't feel like she needed to listen to me or do as she was asked or told. She believed that things were going to move according to her plan and no one else's.

No. Nah ah. Not in my house. I'll be damned. Over my dead body and trust me I finally felt as though I had a lot of life left.

You're going to school and or you're working. There's no way you're just going to run the streets and be all high and mighty with an attitude. She needed to understand that she was in for the lesson of a lifetime and that it was a lifetime process. This was nothing she was going to learn overnight. Yet I was only Mommy and I had only too been a teenage parent, so to her what I had to say surely didn't matter. All she translated everything I said into was: I was only telling her what to do.

There were times our communication would be okay. Then there were times it was rockier than the jagged mountainside. Lord knows I've never seen a mountain with a smooth side. There were times she still played the disappearing game; I don't think she realized how not knowing where she was killed me more and more every moment that went by.

How every time the phone rang or I got a knock on the door my heart would stop. I'm sure I even stopped breathing thinking the worst news was about to come from the other side. Not knowing if your child is safe, outdoors or indoors, if they're dead or alive, beat in a gutter, eating, being pimped out and prostituted, out of the streets and or just okay. That is surely a feeling no parent should have to experience. Yet I overstand agony, stress, depression, anxiety, insomnia and eating disorders. When it came to knowledge through experience I was a jack of all things yet a master to none.

I refused to walk around wearing my life for the world to see. I didn't need to be looked at as though there was a need for a pity party. I refused to walk around looking as beat up as my life had become. It was nobody's business so why the hell would I advertise. So I walked around looking as though nothing more than the "norm" was going on, if there is such a thing as "norm".

19

Yet while this was going on I still had two other children at home. I couldn't forget to share my time and positive loving energy with them. With all this chaos that was engulfing me I had to practice balance. When I didn't know who to turn to, where to go or what to do I ate. Because of my confusion in life I began to find myself feeling negative and thinking negative thoughts. I found myself feeling sick with disgust. I was disgusted with my life, my choices and my present situation. The negative feelings were beginning to consume me. Deep down inside I knew this was all wrong and there had to be better times to come.

I became bitter and angry with life and all that was going on it. I was constantly yelling and my patience was worn thin and transparent. I had no tolerance for anything. My anger always seemed to be missed directed. I'd feel bad after and sometimes have this long drawn out apologetic conversation in my head that never seemed to be heard by anyone except me. The words could never find their way to part my lips and even with that failure it progressed my stress. I was not a me that I wanted to deal with, be with or let alone be. Yet I felt as though that was my dead end. I felt as though at that time my present situation was my life's final destination and I was doomed to be in what felt like the pits of hell to me.

I had to get in touch with myself because I was losing myself while I was chasing everything and everyone else. I couldn't control my thoughts, feelings or actions. I was quick to react to nonsense and it felt as though I was surrounded by nothing but nonsense. I had to find one thing to focus on. My life was in a whirlwind and my thoughts where the substance circulating around the center of the tornado. They weren't good.

I decided I would begin to try and prioritize the events in my life according to urgency. My daughter was expecting there was nothing to do except wait and maintain appointments until it was delivery time. As for the additional issues that would arise with her or any of my other children I'd deal with them as they came. Priority was to take care of the BS that was going on with this house that I was living in and to address the landlord issues. So I decided that I needed to focus on that because it was not safe and I was about to lose the little bit of sanity that I had left.

I began to videotape the things that were going on in the house because I didn't know if I needed it for court or something. I would report these things and many other things to the landlord and he'd never respond. However, he would be sure to come around or send someone to collect the rent on the first of every month. Plus he was sure to come around to do little things around the property when I wasn't home.

The town stayed involved with the fact that there were so many violations and they were hazardous. Once the landlord failed to do the repairs the town came in and gave me a short time to move out before they condemned the property because of the structural hazards and other violations. It was devastating to say the least. Dodging nails as the boarded up windows and trying to pack up last minute things, scrambling around the house trying not to leave anything of value or importance. However through all the chaos and hustle and bustle I found myself leaving quite a bit behind and losing part of my life all over again.

I was able to find a vacant house just on the other side of town. The house originally was for sale. Yet I was blessed that the landlord had decided he would rent it to me; for now. I had to make previsions for moving there with my now bit of a larger family into a bit of a smaller space with my whole less of a pocket full of money.

Things always turned out to be some kind of obstacle, hurdle or struggle. I was always feeling tested. Was it karma? Had I done that many things wrong in the past or past life that I was paying for it now? Was someone out to get me and wishing bad luck on me? Was I being punished for something I did or hell didn't do? There were so many questioned that clouded my mind, body and soul. I felt myself getting sick from being stressed with worry. I knew that I deserved to feel better than this and only I had control of that. It was going to be a process, I decided I was going to go through it and get it started.

I needed to take time to breathe. I needed to take time for myself and be by myself. Spending time with yourself doesn't have to be a lonely time. It could be some of the best time you ever spend quality wise. Get to know yourself. Your strengths and weaknesses, what your skills and abilities are; know what you bring to the table. Enhance your finer points, educate yourself and expand your knowledge on both new and old topics. There's nothing wrong with reinventing the wheel or yourself, think about how the apps on your phone get updated every time you turn around.

Think about it. Why not upgrade or update your life, literally? So that's what I did after I revisited some points in my life. I focused on my strengths and my weaknesses. I than decided I would take time to strengthen my weakness so I could only have lesser strengths. I decided I was no longer going to feed into the negatives. I would develop my strengths all around. This was going to take practice and disciple. I had to think why not invest as much in myself as I had in so many others? Didn't I too deserve the best that I had? You damn right! I did!

Now all the while that life was happening I was eating. I was eating because I was sad, overwhelmed, happy, celebrating, depressed or because I could finally get a meal. Either way my life began to be consumed by food. Pints of ice cream on the late night, chips and dip, soda by the liters, pizza pies, hero sandwiches, cakes and candy basically whatever I wanted whenever I wanted with no concern. In all honesty until I started to pay attention to what I was doing, did I really finally realize what I was doing to myself. I had to step out of the frame to look at the whole picture.

20

There were three major incidences that bought my weight issue to my attention and I am going to share them with you. My daughters were about 10 and 11 and they came home from dance wanting to show me a routine they had learned. Not only did they want to show me they wanted me to do it with them.

Being the mother that I was, I responded okay without hesitation. As they were teaching me the steps, my daughter would ask me: what was this noise she kept hearing over the music when we would do the steps together? I told her I didn't know what she was talking about. When I finally realized the sound she was referring to I decided I'd sit this out and just watch them dance instead. On the inside I was so embarrassed; I was so torn and heartbroken. The sound that she was referring to was the sound of my stomach slapping against my thighs as I tried to do the dance with them. If anyone knows the dance it was the "heel toe". Yup there are just certain things I shouldn't have been doing and that were certainly one of them. After they finished I praised them; then I retreated to my room and silently cried a long cry.

The second situation occurred a few years later. I went to the doctor and after he asked me to get on the scale, he wrote in my chart **morbidly obese** woman and I lost it. I was enraged and I asked him: How you gonna call me morbidly obese yet not even tell me about it? Not even give me anything to do about it? I was crushed and disgusted not only with my weight however with my choice in physicians as well.

When all he could do was stand there and stare at me as though it wasn't him that prescribed me the cakes and sodas, I left the office knowing I had decisions to make. So I made the executive decision to change my life and my doctor. However, I am human and I am a big enough person to admit that I procrastinated with the changing my life part.

So my final wakeup call was one early morning I was lying in bed and needed to get up to use the bathroom. As I tried to get up I felt so heavy. I remember trying to sit right up and struggled. As I tried to swing my legs over the side of the bed to sit up, I couldn't. I literally had to grab my thigh and roll my leg one over the other. I was actually rolling out of bed. Ain't this about a blimp? After this process which felt like it took forever, I sat on the edge of the bed and just cried. I had children that needed me and I wanted to be there for them and active with them. I had to do better if I expected things to get better.

21

In life, when you really want something you may find that you have to be persistent. Trust me whatever it is if you really want it, you will get it. Be willing to fight for what you need and want, the way you would fight for someone else. Learn to love yourself. Know that you matter and you deserve the love that you give to others.

Love yourself first. Love yourself so that when someone sees you they know how to love you too. You can be the one to set the ground rules and guidelines to how people respond to you and how they treat you. Be confident in your decisions. Have the confidence in yourself that you want others to have in you. Don't let road blocks stop you. Do not allow the feeling of defeat to set in, there are always options. Prime example: When I went to change my doctor, the doctor that I found didn't take my insurance. So I had to find out what insurance he did take and then change my insurance. That became an issue because of enrollment dates however I was determined and I got it done.

I began seeing this amazing doctor, Dr. Dominick Riina, a plastic surgeon. We discussed weight loss options and he asked me what I had already tried. I had already tried everything orthodox and unorthodox. From not eating, diet pills, combination of diet pills and diet products, laxatives, slim shakes, lemonade diets, doctor diets, online diets, my own diets etc. etc. etc.

During the process of finding the new doctor, getting the insurance changed and going to the appointment I had tried so much more. I tried everything from more diet pills, to diet guru advice, weight watchers, and personal trainers, diets you could eat, diets you could drink, this diet, that diet and every diet under the sun. I even considered liposuction which is what got me the best advice ever. The fact is that when it came to liposuction my money doesn't flow like that; I just felt hopeless and as if I had no other options. So I had no choice but to move forward on this venture in a more professional approach because my ways alone weren't working.

Dr. Dominic Riina was such a blessing. He was so encouraging and supportive even if I wasn't seeing him for plastic surgery. He is a doctor that truly has concern for his patients.

After speaking with my primary care doctor we decided that I should have a consultation with a bariatric specialist and a nutritionist. That was the first step to the beginning of my new journey. I was referred to make appointments with Dr. Dominick Gadaleta and the nutritionist Nicolette Pace. The nutritionist was amazing. Nicolette really wanted to know me and I really needed to be honest with not only her yet with myself; if this was truly going to work. I had to be honest about my feelings, my situations, my past and my present as well as the foods and drinks that I consumed. I had to open up about everything down to chewing gum, a mint or a cup of water.

That I must say was no easy task yet I must admit it was cleansing and rewarding when I did it. I got some advice on things that I had never considered before. I was able to get another perspective on my situation. Think of life like a rubrics cube every now and again you need to look at things on different angles to see just where it might line up. And when it doesn't line up you try it another way; there are always options. You repeat these steps until the puzzle is solved. Be consistent, be patient, allow yourself time to heal and always keep it real. Know that before you lie to others you are lying to yourself. Why? If they can't handle the truth that's on them; not you. You need to live with yourself so be honest and real always. As they say keep it a 100!

Being 100% honest is so important. We have a tendency to mask our pain in such a way that we rewrite the situation to better cope with it or at times we try to push it so far back we forget about it. That's not healing that is only burying the issue temporarily. Know that a great amount of the things we go through; people wouldn't believe unless they were there. So know that even though your situation may be unique to you it isn't all that rare. You never know who you could be helping if you ever decided to open up and share. It could be in a support group, one to one therapy, your barber, the bartender, a neighbor, a good friend, your parents, or your spouse, meditate on it and perhaps become a speaker to share it with many at once; whatever you do keep your mental health as clean as your physical health. You have one body, one mind and one soul they all need to be loved and taken care of accordingly. You owe it to yourself to love yourself and do the best for you that you can do.

No matter the obstacles that are in your way, know you can overcome everything! Think about it: if you're reading this, to date you are already at a 100% success rate. Don't give up now, why taint it? Remember the only limitations you truly have are the limits you set for yourself.

So, I went to see the bariatric specialist and discussed everything about me. It was such a release being able to be so honest about things in my life and not feel like I needed to keep them a secret. I realized I may have endured things alone yet I am not the only one in life that has had to endure these "types" of things. Since I had already gone through this practice of being open and honest it was becoming easier the more I had to do it and face me. Practice, practice and more practice. No matter what you're practicing it will make it easier and possibly damn near perfect. Look at #WontHeDoIt!!

The doctor and I discussed my options and then he gave me a laundry list of things to get done. I looked at that list feeling a bit defeated. All I wanted was to lose weight already! All this extra stuff I felt was so unnecessary. Seeing all types of specialist and psychiatrist just to lose weight at first didn't make sense. I so didn't understand things at the start of my journey yet the understanding I gained about myself during this journey was amazingly priceless.

I am so glad that this doctor is a thorough doctor. How much better I feel knowing myself inside and out. From psych evaluations to all types of medical clearances, I used each experience to get to know myself better and to be able to write the next chapter of my life rather than to just be a spectator and watch my life happen. I needed to be able to narrate my story in such a way that it made sense to me.

No one can make you feel inferior without your consent. You need to know yourself and what you stand for. Be able to set your own standards and boundaries. If you don't set boundaries than others do not know their limitations; certain situations require structure. You are the architect of your temple. In order to build it to last you must ensure you know what it needs to withstand what life has in store. You may not know the specifics, however once you know yourself and are specific with the Universe; understand the Law of Attraction says something like what you put out there has to come back to you. Be great and be positive. Be sure to build your foundation on the strengths that are necessary for your growth and your life, the rest will come. Take time for you, it's not being selfish it's necessary.

You're words are your verbs. Think positive, speak positive and be positive. I know this may sound a little cheesy just try it. When you wake up in the morning just say Thank you. Be thankful for a night of sound rest, be thankful for seeing another day, be thankful for your family, thankful for the sun, thankful for the job you have, thankful for basically whatever your heart and mind deserves to give thanks for. Once you have given thanks you'll feel a smile inside that might creep on out to the outside and watch how much brighter your day can be.

You set the tone of your day. Don't allow others to dictate how you should feel. There will always be circumstances that may try to pull you into their chaos. You can bet your last red cent that there will always be a situation or circumstance, that's life. It's how you react, how you handle it and the amount and type of energy you put into it that will make or break it for you. Be strong and stand your ground; you could either try to pull them into your peace or just turn and walk away. You make the best choice for you. You are responsible for your feelings and your actions. Keep them positive and make them count.

22

So I completed the list of appointments and medical clearances. That took me about 6 months or longer. Either way, I stuck to it. I stayed consistent and committed to my goal. It was now time to meet the doctor again. To my surprise I was doing great despite the fact that life was constantly happening. Life is constantly happening otherwise we wouldn't be living. Life is a rollercoaster so just buckle up and hold on. The ups and downs and the twist and turns come at a moment's notice. We just need to be aware that they are going to happen and deal with them as they come, not before they come. Try not to wish negativity and chaos into existence. Look forward to enjoying every moment and every second for you can never get it back once it's gone. Make your life count.

I had managed to lose a few pounds not many however some was better than none. Plus some loss was always better than a gain in my case. I was headed in the right direction; the way I looked at it. There's always a bright side to look at in a situation. Dr. Gadaleta and I began to discuss my options. There was the lapband, the gastric bypass or the sleeve.

The lapband procedure was a device that was surgically placed around the stomach to make the stomach pouch smaller. This would assist me with eating smaller meals, slowing down the process when I ate and help me to make better food choices. This device was reversible as to where they could remove it after some time if I wanted it removed. Also the lapband could be adjusted by the doctor if I felt as though I couldn't eat enough or if I felt that I was eating too much.

There was a port to be located under the skin that they could locate by touch yet they would use x-ray to locate it precisely. They would then inject the port with a saline solution that would fill a balloon located inside the ring that is around the stomach. If the lapband appeared to be too tight they would use the same procedure to locate the port however they would insert the needle into the port to extract the saline fluid out to loosen the band. All this is done after the doctor uses a local anesthetic to numb the area around the port.

The sleeve on the other hand was a surgical procedure whereas they actually cut your stomach to resemble a "sleeve" which served the same purpose as the lapband. However this was a little more invasive and permanent. Think of your stomach as a kidney bean. Imagine the stomach or this kidney bean on a side view. In order for the procedure of the sleeve to take place, they surgically remove the lower "pocket portion" of the stomach. Suturing the incision, your stomach will now resemble the sleeve of your shirt instead of a kidney bean. With this process it would assist with portion control and the rate at which I ate food as well.

Then finally there was the gastric bypass which to me was way too invasive. In short they were going to rewire my plumbing system and I didn't think that was the right choice for me. So I did the research and had to come to an informed decision. I weighed all my options (no pun intended) and went with what was best for me at that time.

I opted for the lapband; to me it was the least invasive and I could have it removed for any reason at any time. The other 2 proceeds are pretty permanent and I wasn't ready for such an invasive procedure. Truth be told, I knew that I wanted to be a #SizeSatisfied, however I was also a little afraid to lose the weight. I had gotten a bit comfortable being the size I was. Not to the degree that I absolutely wanted to remain overweight, just enough to know that I was afraid of looking sickly or strange if I lost the weight. What was my skin going to look like if I lost the weight? Would it sag or snap back? Can the doctors fix it and it get covered by insurance or will it be an out of pocket expense? I wanted it to be slow and progressive yet a bit instantaneous. It was such an emotional rollercoaster ride.

Another part of me was afraid of what people would think or what they would say. How would they react to me having surgery? Losing weight? Will they support me or put me down? Will they judge me? What if I go through all of this for nothing? What if this doesn't work? Will I like my new body? Will it look like such and such? Etc. etc. etc.... The concerns and thoughts were endless.

However I had to realize this was all about me. I walked this walk or should I say I sashayed with this wobble long enough. I wanted to be a #SizeSatisfied regardless of what that was. I wasn't looking to be a supermodel; I just wanted to be a #SizeSatisfied. It was my choice, my chapter, my life, my story and I was on my way.

So with that we scheduled the date for my pre surgical testing and then we scheduled my surgery date. I was in a whirlwind of emotions. I was excited to begin the new road to a healthier better life, I was anxious and I was nervous. I was on my way to a #SizeSatisfied whatever size or weight that might be. I was consciously entering into the unknown and I was ready for anything. I had to hold on to faith, hope and confidence in myself. I was also doing this (physically) all alone. I had my very supportive team of health professionals and the few selected friends who knew my plan. My friends just never knew if and when I was going to actually go through with it.

One of my top concerns about telling people what I was going to do was I was afraid that I would fail. I didn't want to be the one looked at as if I couldn't control myself and my eating habits even with surgery. I wasn't exactly sure if I was ready to be fully accountable for what I did, for what did or didn't take place in the eyes of others. So I mentioned the surgery to very few friends and family with no real details on the procedure. Because ultimately it was about my perspective of my life and I was making this decision because I was ready to make a difference in my life.

23

Day of the surgery came and I had lost a few more pounds. Wooo Whooo yay me! I was already getting myself ready for my life change by changing my eating habits. Making better food choices, eating at better hours of the day, adding vitamins and daily supplements, drinking more water and being more active, I was excited and determined.

In the visits that led up to my surgery I had gone from about 367 lbs. to 330 lbs. Yet I knew I still needed this in order for me to be successful in my weight loss battle. So I got the lapband done in 2006. The surgery went marvelous with no complications and the aftercare was great too.

However the first thing that gave me grief was the gas. I thought the pain was going to kill me. That was when I became best friends with Tums, Pepcid and Gas-X. Once I got that under control and I followed the steps with the proper portions when eating; things were going exceptionally well.

I had to follow a specific diet if this was going to work. It would take me through several food stages. It would start out with a liquid diet for a few days. Then you would graduate to a diet of pureed foods. Pretty much the many stages of baby food until eventually you could eat solid food in small moderate portions. That was the way I had to learn to eat. It was challenging going from a hero to a protein shake yet I know I had a goal and I had to do what it took to keep my eyes on the prize.

Then I realized I needed to also be more active if this process was really going to go full circle. So I began working out a little here and a little there. Nothing crazy like joining a gym or anything, I wasn't ready for an audience. So I would work out in the privacy of my bedroom. I would do little things like leg lifts and arm rotations while I was in the bed. Then I might get a little more creative and adventurous and do dips on the edge of the bed or pushups off the bed during commercial breaks.

Understand that the body just needs to be in motion. The more you move the more you lose. I would also clean the house to my favorite music and dance like no one was watching – at least that is what I prayed. Yet I actually would look forward to these little stolen moments of exercise as if I was doing something forbidden yet oh so rewarding. I would gradually see a difference and for reasons unknown to me I also starting feeling a little happier with myself. Everything was gradually improving in my life. Once I stopped, recalculated my steps and started taking care of the one person that took care of so many others and so many things - ME.

I would begin to see little changes in the way my clothes would fit, my face got a little slender; I lost a neck or two and a few rolls in each of my stomachs. I was eating right and to my surprise these new food choices tasted pretty good too. Actually what I will say to keep things honest is I was eating better and the right portions. I was working out a little more consistently and I was communicating with my support team and health professionals. I kept this up and stayed on track for about 5 years. Within that time I lost about 70-80 lbs.

However due to the amount of weight that I lost I had excessive skin that began to get ulcers and sores between the layers. Due to the medical necessity I had abdominoplasty done in 2011. That's where the amazing Dr. Riina came back into my life. He pointed me in the right direction from the beginning. I was under the impression I wanted to be a #SizeSatisfied so I'll just get plastic surgery. Ummm, I was sadly mistaken.

Life requires work. Sometimes more work than I expected. I couldn't believe and still can't believe that I work this hard to stay this broke. That left liposuction as I've said before: as no option. However, Dr. Riina didn't give up on me. He counseled me on several occasions and oh how thankful I am. When I was told that I needed to have this abdominoplasty aka tummy tuck done; I was sure to go to Dr. Riina.

I was cut from hip to hip to remove pounds of skin. When this procedure was complete I was released from the hospital with drains attached to the incisions. All I really recall is this was a painful recovery time.

24

Once I fully recovered I began to really start to enjoy life. My clothes fit in a way that I had never experienced. I felt like I might just fit in clothes in my closet that were what I called "Target Clothes". My "Target Clothes" consisted of those outfits that I had bought, never returned and vowed to get into one day.

I know I'm not alone. I know you all have those "I'm gonna get in you jeans, dress, shorts or tops..." Hell, well no shame in my game, I had outfits. It was a bit strange to me; I might just not only fit into certain clothes however I might just fit into society. Into this thing people called life and living. I felt like a total stranger to myself. I had options that had never been options for me. I had someone new to get to know – Me. I was ready to enjoy the process; not even looking for the end result.

I wasn't being selfish I was just doing what was necessary. I didn't want to make any excuses. I had procrastinated in my life long enough. My time for change was now and I was ready to face reality and embrace it.

It's funny; my kids noticed my changes and at times were unsure how to react. I get it now yet I didn't get it then. I couldn't give them an explanation to something that I myself didn't understand. I just went with the flow. I was not only changing physically. I began to change and grow mentally.

Prior to my choice of change I was under the impression that in life you are who you are. That is true and not so true all in the same breath. You are who you mold yourself to be. Remember you are a human not a leopard that never changes its spots.

There were many times I'd surprise myself at the way I would react to a situation so I know I confused so many others. The way I handled and reacted to things became so different. It was all through research and practice. The research and practice of the desire to be a better person, to learn that new dance called relax and just enjoy the process.

Let me explain the best way I can briefly... As a heavier woman that wasn't too sure of who she was, where she was going, what life had in store and how she was going to do it... I was not only overweight I was stressed, overwhelmed, depressed, overworked and underpaid. I was angry very often more so than not. I would stop myself from trying things, out of fear of failing. It was so bad I had felt I had failed before I would even attempt something. I was always so frustrated I yelled, I screamed, I kept an attitude and put my guards up completely.

I was unable to communicate this feeling and so it came out with me being negative about everything and anything all the time. They didn't get it, they didn't like it hell truth be told neither did I. I just couldn't explain at that time what I didn't understand. I wasn't angry at them I was angry at my situation. I was angry at the poor choices I felt that I made. I was as angry as a wild animal backed into a corner. I just didn't know better to do better until I took time to know me. Then I had to learn to do better by me; so I could do better for them and anyone else.

So I worked on myself mentally, physically, emotionally and spiritually. I took the time to try new foods and eat better, workout and be more active in life. I began to try things like yoga, meditation, learning about chakras and energies, crystals and healing stones, positivity and the Law of Attraction and so much more. I took time to educate me and to further my education.

I finally even joined a gym. I would work out anywhere from 3-4 days a week from an hour to 2 hours per session. I would do a combination of cardio exercises, lift weights and calisthenics. Things were going great. I was living a healthier lifestyle and I loved the results. I was working myself to a #SizeSatisfied and loving what I was learning about me, my life and instilling in me and my family in the process.

The process is different for each and every one of us. Learn to be patient with yourself. The things you wish to change didn't manifest itself in a day. So take your time and step out of the frame to look at the picture to gain a different perspective of how things are, how they can be and what your options are to get you there. Then prioritize your options and work your way down the list. Life isn't a dead end street. You are the construction, road and maintenance crew of your life so do some demolition and make way for multiple lanes, avenues and folks in the road etc. that you have the blueprint to develop. Your options can be limitless. Be creative. Show yourself that you still have that creative side in you with the experience to transform it to aid any situation. Never give up. There are no excuses.

After about 5 or 6 years, I hit a roadblock and I plateaued. I found that no matter what I did I wasn't losing any more weight and there would be times I seemed to be gaining. So you know what time it was; time to go back to the drawing board.

I wasn't going to believe I couldn't continue to do better and be better. I saw the potential for my life to improve. I still had work to do I hadn't reached my #SizeSatisfied. Prior to making these decisions about my weight and my life I had little to no hope that things would ever be better or that my days could be brighter. I was certain I wanted the better and brighter so I did some research and decided to consult with Dr. Gadaleta and his wonderful medical team again.

I consulted with my wonderful team of health and surgical professionals and I decided I wanted to get the lapband removed and have an alternative surgery done called the sleeve. The lapband as I stated was reversible, it could be removed however the sleeve is a little more of an invasive procedure that has the same premise. The point of both of these surgeries is to help me with my eating portions and aid me in controlling when I felt full and needed to push away from the table or plate. That's pretty much it in a nutshell.

25

Knowing that I still needed to eat well and work out if I wanted to see positive results I was ready to advance on my journey. These surgeries in no way are magic solutions to losing weight. They are simply tools for you to build a foundation for your stepping stones to a healthier you. If you want the surgery to work for you; you have to put in the work for you. It is not as if you get the surgery and then poof you're skinny. Following the guidelines for portion control, exercise, water intake, being active and living a positive life are all essential to being a #SizeSatisied regardless of the path you choose to get there. Surgery isn't for everyone and I am in no way telling anyone that this is or isn't the way to go. This is solely the chapter of my life to getting to my #SizeSatisfied.

So in July of 2013 I got the lapband removed and the sleeve was done. Just to recap a bit. The sleeve procedure is basically this: picture the stomach in the shape of a kidney bean. Looking at the kidney bean on a side angle, the long way, the bottom half is removed and the remaining portion resembles that of a sleeve.

I can still realistically eat whatever I choose to eat however the bigger question then becomes: what results am I really looking for? So because by now I know that if I want better I need to do better, I needed to step things up a notch. With the fact that the lapband had already helped me to condition myself to eat smaller meals, transitioning from the lapband to the sleeve had very little adjustments I needed to make to my eating habits. This procedure just required less outside maintenance from doctors and was more on me to make the differences I needed for my life. I needed to be accountable and responsible for my choices and actions. Moving forward I had to make the right decisions.

With that being said I couldn't lie to myself and say I didn't eat this or that. Or say that I just would eat one when I would certainly have five. I couldn't say I had my fruits, veggies and protein for the day on that taco slice I wolfed down with garlic knots and an orange soda. Nor that my healthy snack and exercise was the chocolate covered almonds I ate and finished while watching the workout video I bought yesterday. How about because I carried in all the groceries that was now considered to be my cardio and I don't need to go to the gym. The excuses only catch up with you. In order for you to see results you have to be doing something. I had to stop doing nothing in order to see something.

So the surgery and recovery went exceptionally well. I was on my path to my new found life. I was at a point in my life where I was taking the next necessary steps to reach my #SizeSatisfied and finding myself in the process. It's funny there are many reasons that I didn't speak to more people about my choices as I was making them.

In all honesty one of my top reasons was I was afraid to fail. I was afraid to fail with everyone knowing my goal and then be accountable for my failure and my lack of effort in moments of weakness. I didn't want to have to answer to anyone or explain myself to anyone either. And for those that did know my decisions when I found myself slipping I would also find myself pulling away from everyone and everything. I'd become a bit withdrawn. I found myself being a professional loser yet wasn't ready to admit to myself let alone to anyone else that I assumed didn't already know.

However I'd then remind myself that this journey is a rollercoaster ride and there will certainly without a doubt be ups and downs. Success is never permanent unless you wish to obtain nothing else and failure is never final unless you quit. There will be trials and tribulations and test that can be turned into testimonies. No need to be a victim when you can be victorious. This is what life is all about. Choices! Options!

Knowing that in every good day there were blessings and in every day that I struggled with there were plenty of lessons. Know that every situation and circumstance that I have ever encountered has made me who I am today. I wouldn't change any of that for anything in the world. For I know that in order to truly appreciate being up I've had to experience the downs. In order to find my limits and boundaries many lines had to be crossed. Just like the ying and the yang there is light in the dark and in the dark there is light.

Now I'm on a roll and ready to conquer the world. Ok perhaps not the world just yet, at least conquer my weight. So I made a vow, a commitment, to myself first with the little things in life then gradually adding things on.

26

I remained consistent and persistent. I challenged myself with every step that I took whether it was backwards or forwards. On days that I missed a workout or didn't make the best food choices I had consequences for myself. Just as in the days that I completely followed through or went above and beyond my daily goals I'd reward myself within reason.

Always being sure to leave room for the next reward, I put together daily routines that had substance to my ultimate goal. I'd do fun things so that I enjoyed the process and not looked at it as though it was a job or unwanted task. I wanted to look forward to taking care of me and with persistent practice. Now I find I do it without much thought. Be creative and add variety. Variety is the spice of life they say, so use it. FYI: Spice is great for boosting the metabolism by the way.

No need for things to get boring. It's your routine mix it up and what you will find is your life and your body will thank you. You'll find yourself using mental and physical muscles in a way that you never have. Be careful though you may find yourself amazing yourself and that is an awesome feeling. Life is like a kaleidoscope it's full of amazing and phenomenal sights, feelings and experiences and no one experience is exactly like another. The variables are forever changing.

With that being said I finally started to use the gym membership that I've been paying for about a year or two. I also began to go to a workout class at the local community center. In addition, I made appointments to work out with this amazing personal trainer Sarah Klima. I scheduled my workouts, my meals according to my day, I had preplanned what to eat at what mealtimes and prepared most of my meals for myself on the go.

For the times that I didn't bring my meals from home and I knew that I would be going out to eat, I would look up the menu choices in advance so that I could have a pretty good idea as to what I was having without being overwhelmed with thinking I was making a rapid decision. I incorporated more water consumption into my day which helped me feel full as well as hydrated. Being hydrated helped during times of exercise as well as aided in keeping my skin to look clear and radiant. Water is something so simple and has a multitude of uses and benefits.

I started educating myself on fitness and great nutrition by visiting my local health food stores & fitness centers speaking with them about vitamins, minerals, food and drinks that did different jobs for the body. I spoke with my nutritionist, Nicolette, to stay on top of the best things that I needed specifically in my daily diet and I spoke with my doctor, Dr. Gadaleta, to ensure that I was doing great with my level of physical activity.

I will even admit that due to multiple stressors in my life there's been a time or two that I have put myself in therapy. Yes therapy, mental health is just as important if not more important than physical health. I needed to remain in the right frame of mind. M'onique said it best "I could've been your cellmate..." Because only the Universe knows just how angry I was. We all know that we can do foolish things in the midst of anger so I was also at times a bit unpredictable and not necessarily in the best way.

Everyone needs a place to vent; sometimes with the expectation of advice and sometimes just to let off steam. Being a single parent I didn't date much so I didn't have an adult counterpart to confide in. So I made sure that my health was being properly nurtured from the inside out. I needed to ensure that the thoughts in my mind were clear and positive so that the feelings I felt were amazing and progressive and that could ensure that my actions were productive and plenty.

The body is a machine that works altogether. Mind, Body and Soul must be positive and forever building on knowledge and skills to ensure that it's always in the best health possible. Please do not misunderstand me; I am not saying I am happy and blissful 100% of the time. However what I am saying is I know me enough to know when I am no longer being positive and pull myself back into my own peace and tranquility.

I also will admit that I have a tendency to slip up and "eat what I want". I'm human dang nabit. As long as I am aware and I take the time to care I know it was only for a second. That next second or minute can be used to do better and make a wiser decision. Everyone has that chance for change. The first step may be a leap even; just know that once you take the first, the second the third; before you know it you're walking in the park of Life. Even with that being said in every park someone walks their dog and they are sure to leave a mess; so just watch your steps.

I know you can do it. I did it and I am still doing it. I have so much more work to do and I see myself being successful. I will reach my goals because I won't quit. In time all things change and since time stands still for no one; know that transformation in your life is inevitable. Whether it's negative or positive that is up to you. Positive energy is just as contagious as negative energy. Be the change you want to see in your life. Set and be your own example.

You can rewrite your story from any point in your life and tell that story the way, you, the narrator and creator only can. You are the best for this position so take hold to this position and handle it well. Know your position and your job description and do it well - for you. You are the captain of your ship, the writer of your story and the narrator of your production.

Don't get me wrong I am human you know there are times that I tend to slip up so to speak. I do still eat out and I still snack on things that aren't the best choices however I realize and then I get back on track. There is always every second, every minute, every hour and every day that gives you the opportunity to start on a clean canvas. Whether this analogy is used for food or for anything else it works.

You always have the chance to be a better you. Challenge yourself sometimes. Step out of your comfort zone. I dare you to get uncomfortable. Do something out of the norm. I did just that. I challenged myself and I surprised the hell out of me. I did the Polar Bear plunge with the sands on the beach covered in a thick comforter of snow, I skydived from 13,500 feet out of a perfectly good airplane, I made it to see age 40 and was able to wear a gown for the first time in life. I only see greater challenges and success to come. Dream a dream you've never dreamed. Know that it's okay to dream big. Remember only you set your limits.

Don't allow your circumstances, situations or environments to define you. These things can change at a moment's notice so realize in life so can you. Keep it positive; life is like a coin and every coin has a flip side. Slow down just a little and learn to breathe. Life can and will be challenging. Would it be life if it wasn't a challenge? Struggles make us stronger, hurdles make us clever and obstacles keep us active. It's all a matter of perception.

Give yourself time and space to heal. You deserve that. Be real with yourself because that's the one person you can't run from. Know that if you are not okay you cannot do for others even if that is your will. Tell people "...I need this time for me so that I can be there for you..." that may open them up a little more to a better understanding. You are human you have feelings to.

Don't lose yourself trying to find someone or something else. Surround yourself with like-minded people. People that share common interest, goals, hobbies, views etc. Be consistent with including yourself in the equation and not just solving everyone else's.

Communicate your needs so others will know. We can't walk around assuming that people are aware of what you require in and for your life. Communication is key. Know that all things change so strive to surpass yourself every chance you get. You should always be your greatest competition. The best way to be successful is to set a goal, see the process through from beginning to end and reach your goal.

Stimulate your mind, internalize your positive thoughts and present them through actions. Life offers endless possibilities, learn how to get out of your own way and not block your successes and blessings. Getting out of my own way has been a process and I'm not finished yet. I am forever pushing forward...

Know that all things good and bad make us who we are. If any of those elements were to change then you better believe that who we are, who we've become or who we will be has the ability to change too. Nothing is ever set in stone unless you put it there and quit. Find your niche. Be creative and adventurous. Life has so much to offer so be open to the new and unknown and be observant. Some things are for you and somethings are not. Be true to yourself and remember to show yourself love.

27

In life there will always be hurdles things will always be happening. Like tides in the water wading at the shore they are just keeping us a little off balance. However, it's a fact that they both make us think quick on our feet.

You hold the blueprint to your life, there is no need to conform. Stand out and be original. You are the only you in this world. Find yourself. Be yourself and be the best you that you can be. Live, love and laugh be goofy at times and be sure to balance work and play. Know inside and out that it is okay to be you! Know that you have it naturally; even an impersonator has to study and rehearse.

Be committed from start to finish. Know that the end of the road only comes when you draw the line. Why draw the line when there is no limit to life? When you have reached the level of success you aimed for, know that there are other goals to set and other successes to accomplish. For this I am forever thankful.

My youngest daughter is always telling me that she is finding her inner sparkle. Truth be told she was teaching me a thing or two. I had lost my sparkle some time ago. Life and its many trials and tribulations had put out my flame. My spark was dwindling and then situations and people just kicked dirt all over it. I felt as though that was it and there was no other way for my life or its circumstances. Once I remembered that I too did deserve the right to live and be happy, I had to look for a way to clear the dirt and at least get my spark back to see what wildfires would start.

I challenge myself daily even several times in a day at times. Now I challenge you to do greater things in your life. Whether it's your weight, family, substance, a struggle or situation. Take the time to change the perspective in which you've been looking at it and find the options that lie below the surface.

Don't give up on your life for you are the only one that can keep your life going forward. You have to make steps to run into possibilities. Things are not going to just come to you. If you want it you'll get it.

Since I have found myself, I see things in such a different light. The sky looks bright to me even on cloudy days, I hear the chirps of the birds clear as a cloudless sunny day and my sense of smell and desire to see beauty in all things has also heightened. My shoulders seem to not feel so heavy, my posture has improved, the way that I walk has such a confidence that it even surprises me a time or two. I walk into a room and the energy that I give off makes people feel as though they need to know me.

Seriously every day is a day that I seem to find out new and exciting things about myself. My patience use to be null and void. I would be ready to yell and scream damn near throw a tantrum because things were going so disarray. I felt as though I was living under a very grey cloud, I would tell folks if it wasn't for bad luck I'd have no luck. If something had a .0001% chance of going wrong I'd be in that percentile and that was a guarantee.

You know how they say that lightning never strikes in the same place twice well I've proven that theory wrong. Seems like my name is bullseye because I always get hit right on target. You know life is always going to be happening. You just need to know that and be able to accept it. Not dwell on or allow it to control your mind and your actions. Just know it and be aware, then move about in such a way that every step you take is a step in a direction that makes you happy.

The steps that you take will enhance your self-worth and rebuild your life with the substances that will make you the remarkable unique person that you were put in this Universe to be. There is no need to worry because the things that we worry about will be there when it's time for the worry to be addressed. Live in the now. Enjoy this moment at this time. Remember the feeling so you can relive it and upgrade it.

Many times I felt as though I was on autopilot and I just allowed myself to "go with the flow". I went with the flow so often I could go with the flow in my sleep. My life was so routine that if I had a stalker they'd get bored waiting for me at my next stop. There was no real adventure, no real direction and no real spark. I always just expected the worst and prepared for the worser. I never believed that things in the life of this poor little girl from a small town in the projects had a chance.

I didn't feel as if I deserved a chance. Not that I was a bad a person, I just felt that there were so many better people than me that deserved a chance. However I woke up when my life started lightening up and I had this epiphany that I too deserved better. I deserved whatever it was that I needed and that I wanted in this life. I would just have to be willing to work a little smarter and not harder to get it.

I always thought that different things in my life required much hard work. And that even with this hard work, it was only practice for more hard work. I felt this way mainly because people would always tell me that practice makes perfect and everything happens for a reason. Yet at those times in my life, I saw no reason whatsoever for the things that were going on. Every answer in my life seemed to be no. The only time it seemed to be yes was when I would say it or if it was something that would benefit the other person. So I felt as though I was only in practice for more rough times.

I had to realize that I was only beneficial until the benefits ran out. People both good and bad have their own intentions. Many times I have encountered the negative of the two. Negative energy would make it so hard for me to distinguish when it was a positive force or energy that was entering my life. There were many times I found myself standing in my own way. I was blocking my blessings and my great fortune. I felt that everyone was out to get me; to use me. I felt that with all the tattoos that I have, perhaps I missed the one on my face that read: useable material, boo boo the fool, sucker etc. etc. etc. etc.

See I'm a giver by nature. I've had a hard time telling people no. I really have a problem with putting my all out there and expecting that at some time in life someone will do the same for me somewhere down the line. Yet what I had to learn and it was a hard yet useful lesson was "Having less expectations of people and situations will leave you with fewer disappointments in life". I had to learn this because in all my years of waiting and expecting I've been very disappointed. If I can prevent a negative feeling why do something that knowingly will invite it?

People are not going to do as you do. Why? It's simple because they are not you. You are unique you are the only you that will ever be. People can try to duplicate you and they may even imitate you however they will never in life be you. Even identical twins are unique individuals. Think about it, that's an amazing thing about life. You are the only you just as I am the only me. I don't know about you however I would have it know other way. Besides I'm not too certain the world could handle more than one of me... ;-)

Be yourself. If you don't know who you are it's okay. Just don't forget to find yourself. Try to never lose sight of who you are while trying to find someone or something else. Understand that in life growth and change is inevitable regardless of how hard we fight it. When we fight change and try to control it the end result may be devastating.

I have gained an overstanding that in my life things are going to happen. Whether I just let them, make them happen or just watch them happen they are going to happen. I have a choice as to how I respond to what is happening and that's all part of the process. Your reaction is going to either satisfy or upset the action. You at that point decide what outcome you are looking for. If you are looking for conflict and chaos than perhaps you will find yourself reacting in a negative way or in way with little thought behind it. Or perhaps you will take the time you need to find the solution to that situation in that moment that will satisfy you in a way that little or no negativity can phase that moment in time.

We all need to learn to be in the moment. That is when you can really enjoy life. We all have concerns, worries, bills, struggles, differences, situations and issues that plague our lives. We don't need to harp on these things though as if that is the only thing that exists. Every coin has two sides; even a doubled headed coin. So if you are in a situation and not really sure how to move forward, there is no rule that says you can't take a step back first to look at things from a different angle. To take the time that you need to find the best response for you in that moment.

Seriously, know that even as I write this I have issues that plague me, bills that are due and deadlines to be met. How many of you wake up peeking at the cable box to see if you have those dashes where the time once was or if perhaps it now has a message scrolling across the LED window reading : "For Service Call Your Local Cable Provider". Even better where are all my folks that creep? Creep up on your house after a long day at work to see if your outside motion light comes on so you know your electric ain't cut off. I know I'm not alone.

Look life will always throw you curve balls. It's all about your stance at the plate and how you swing the bat; if you choose to swing at all. Know that what is good for me may not be good for you. I do not live a cushiony life with no stressors or issues. It's quite the contrary my dears. My life has made little to no sense whatsoever, however it's my life. Those events have made me into the me, the outcast, the black sheep or the whatever you want to call me that I am not. Know that it's not what you call me it's what I answer to. Also know and realize that I am not my circumstances or situations.

Your time is your life. You have to use both of them wisely because you can never get either one of them back once they are gone. I hear people say Y.O.L.O. You Only Live Once. Well I have to disagree. You only die once. You have the chance to live every day. Don't waste that time and don't take it lightly. Time is precious; enjoy it, cherish it and don't waste it. Construct it in such a way that in time the things that are remembered of you are your greatness.

28

I have come to a crossroad in my life where I am no longer trying to bury my past. I just want to enjoy today and look forward to tomorrow. Funny as it may sound I just recently began dreaming. I began not only dreaming at night yet also I have visions in the day of vivid scenes in my life that I so can't wait to encounter. I see them throughout the day and they make a smile come across my face that many times I don't even anticipate. I feel it in my soul and things begin to shine.

These thoughts sometimes even cause butterflies to start having tag team wrestling matches in my stomach. I feel flushed and all tingly inside. You know what, nobody even has a clue what the source of my happiness is and that's okay. The source of my happiness is me. I'm happy because I make myself happy. I'm happy because I focus on the positive and I use my positive thoughts to receive positive in return.

I don't act this way as though nothing bad can happen. I most definitely do not act this way because adversities haven't taken place. I act this way because I know bad can happen. Knowing these things don't make me better than anyone else knowing this helps me to know myself better than anyone else. By me being in control of my happiness I have control of my life. Never give any one person or thing so much control over you that you have absolutely no control at all. Enable your self-control, be the captain of your ship and the engineer at your controls. It takes practice, practice and more practice.

You may even find that at times you will have to have a conversation or two with yourself to put yourself back on track or to figure out the best solution to a situation. Hey know that talking to yourself every now and again doesn't make you crazy, hell sometimes we all can use a bit of expert advice. The best person to talk to about you is you believe it or not. Take the time for you that you would take for someone else; you can even take a little more. It's not being selfish it is abundantly necessary.

Do for you what you would do for others. Treat yourself; a spa day, manicures and pedicures, a fancy dinner, a movie night, buy yourself something nice (and don't return it), plan a staycation or a vacation whatsoever you do just do it for you. When you start to treat yourself a specific way others will know how to treat you. If there are those that don't follow suit and they seem as though they don't know how to treat you, they can either learn or leave.

You do not by any means have to allow chaos or negativity to live in your space rent free or at a fee. You decide what you allow in your life, so that you can be in control of what you put out of your life. No more oops that slipped. Have so much self-control that people that think they know you will see you now and swear you are acting funny. You just let them know that you are being true to the new you and you aren't acting funny at all. You took some time for yourself to find yourself. Many people are people that learn by example so set the example that you would want them to follow.

Be amongst people that celebrate you and your life not those that go around just tolerating you and your presence. I believe the words of the great Maya Angelou and Mark Twain went something like: You should never make someone a priority when you are just their option.

Know yourself and know your wealth. Many people such as your close friends and family may not understand your desire to change and what your plan is for your life. You should know that attempting to be the picture that everyone else sees you as is like looking at the great works of Pablo Picasso. It may be wonderful to look at and such a sight to see yet too much scrutiny you may begin to think the pieces and colors just don't fit. Trust me. It all works together not just because they do however because it's all about perception. Take a moment to let that simmer. Oh how brilliant.

You are this walk of art with no direction because you have decided to just let go of the reins and just be. You need to be certain not to lose yourself trying to be this great Picasso painting. Let's say you are more of the square type then damn it be the best damn square you can be. Like what you like, do what you do, experience life on the level that you want your life on. Life is limitless. You are the one that either climbs the ladder or you sit at the base and count the steps. Because there are so many steps you may find yourself losing count and having to start over and over and over again. You get so frustrated you decided what the point of even trying is. If you reach this point know that the only place to go from here is up. Take a chance and take a step or two. It's okay to get comfortable being uncomfortable. I did and I am loving it!

This is the point in trying. You can't expect for this moment right now in your life to change until you take the first step in the direction you want to go. You need to take the lead in your life. Seek and find your passion. Even if you need to think back to your childhood when our minds were free and our decisions were fearless. No one says that your inner child has no say. If you think back, Eh em... that's where it all began.

As a child we would think when I grow up I want to be...

We would believe that the sky was the limit and at that time the sky seemed so far away it allowed our dreams to be so vast and highly supplied. No one says that where you are today this is your end. Only you make that possible, and that's when you stop trying. You have the right at any time in your life to rewrite your story.

There's no one direction for your life to go in and there is no one process that will make it work; there are always options. If you think you have run out of options than simply change the angle that you are looking at it. Take a step back or even a few steps and look at things in a different perspective. If you feel that you still aren't sure it's okay to ask the right source for assistance. If all else fails then just Google it or ask SIRI. Nowadays everything is googleable and SIRI has all the answers too.

29

People may look at you like oh my you're acting different and you've changed. Thank them for taking the time to notice and keep up the great work. Of course you've changed were you supposed to remain the same. Think about your life the way you think about your gidgets and gadgets.

All your electronics, data plans and Facebook statuses; every now and again requires an update or an upgrade. You are just as important if not more so upgrade and update you. Give yourself the step up so that when you step out your confidence shines, you feel so good about yourself and what you are doing are for yourself. Find your level of appreciation for your life so others will know what to give you back.

You are in charge of how people treat you. They may think that you are becoming cocky or self-centered. Just let them know it's not that at all its confidence. Know thyself. Take that time so others cannot deter you from your destiny in this life. We all have our own destiny to follow. Along that journey we are going to come across a lot of different people and circumstances. Some are just there to show us and teach us a thing or two. Trust these are going to be both good and bad; positives and negatives. Why? Simple just to keep things balanced on the scale of life.

For me, it's not by any means seeming balanced because most of my hardships seemed to always be so big and so heavy. However, I started to take notice of the little things in my life and I would see just how balanced my life truly is. I needed to step back from my life and be opened minded to visualizing things being better and more stable in my life.

You can start to appreciate the little things in life and build up such a surplus of great things that when things go bad you have your own cushion to fall back on. Create your own surroundings with the tools and skills that you need to prepare yourself for the situations that you may encounter. Yes, I overstand that life is unpredictable however I know that we also have some type of idea as to the hurdles we may have to jump and hills we may have to climb. So be prepared for those things because they will always be there. Life is definitely not a plateau nope sure not a flat line. The flat line only appears when all with this life here is said and done.

You have to keep up the beats of your life. Create a melody that will create so much harmony people can feel the love and confidence you have for yourself and your life. Life is as amazing as you see it. I've gotten into this awesome habit because of a wonderful inspiring person in my life. When people ask me how I am doing I am Wonderful or I am Amazing. For that, to him I must say a deep heartfelt THANK YOU!!

I'm more than just good. I am GREAT! I am AWESOME and AMAZING! When you see the great little things in life you learn to accumulate them in abundance and you smile without even trying. Don't get me wrong I don't have my dream job (it's coming I can taste it), I haven't hit the lotto (because I have more dreams than I have dollars – I won't quit though), I'm not happily married to my best friend (still praying on that), I don't own my own home (yet this is high on my five year plan) etc. etc. etc.

However I did wake up this morning, with a sound body and mind (depends on who you're asking), I have clothes to put on, a way to work, my health, strength, my children, the sun is shining or perhaps it's raining either way I can feel the elements kiss my skin. You see my list of appreciations to me they certainly out way the hurdle and situations that I have yet to conquer.

There is no need to put the energy into worrying as that can be detrimental to your health. Let me deal with the worrisome situation when it approaches not before it arises as if I'm sending out invites. Yes I'm Amazing and prepared for things to only get better. So there is no need for the worries to RSVP.

When you need a way to remind yourself about just how awesome and amazing things are leave yourself reminders. Post a sticky note, make it a screensaver on your phone, tablet, laptop, computer, write it on paper and put it in your pocket or your wallet. It can be a saying, a mantra or just a reminder to breathe in the moments of adversity.

It's great when you have that friend to remind you of how many times you yourself need to be that friend to yourself. Think about it: who is with you more times in the day then they are not? Hint hint: You! You never leave your side. You can talk sense into yourself in a situation without uttering a single word. You can make split second decisions that can change your whole life so just be sure to be your best friend just as you are a friend or best friend to others. It all comes with practice.

You have to sometimes learn to put yourself first; I repeat it is so not being selfish it is necessary. You have to take care of you in order for you to continue to take care of the people and things you take care of before you. You aren't just there to solve the problems and equations. You are most definitely an important part of the equation. You are the variable that seems to never change. Be sure to care for yourself so that the solutions you come across are conducive to the path that you are on.

30

When it comes to paths that we're on they can be planned or they can be on the fly. In my life it has come across as being planned to be on the fly. Some may not make sense of it and to others it just may make all the sense in the world. I've decided that I will not attempt to guide and control what happens and how it happens. What I will control is my reaction to these things that just seem to happen.

I will control and guide the way I administer my solutions to whatever the situation is. Then and only then can I be satisfied with whatever the end result is because I am the one that put out the attempt and it either worked or it didn't. Then I also would have the opportunity to make a different decision from the one that seemed to fail. I will never give up. I will always continue to put forth my best effort with a little extra bringing up the rear.

While life was taking me on this wild ride so many other things starting happening. I got fed up! Fed up with feeling like I was a spectator of my life and I wasn't participating. I was watching things happen to me and not really knowing what to do or how to get out of it. What was I to do to see changes? The type of changes that made sense to my life and what was going on at that moment in time.

I've always been told how smart and talented I've been and I never really knew whether to agree or disagree. I merely offered a thanks figuring that sufficed. I didn't know what to do with this and other compliments that came from people. People are constantly telling me how beautiful I am and do you know I blush every time? Like who me? I decided that if I wanted different I needed to do different.

I was finally seeing more positive than negative. I saw change happening. They were small changes and nothing I thought was important enough to write home about. Nevertheless they were changes and changes for the better. So the first thing I did was I read. Yup that's right I read; I read books, I read things on the internet and I even went back and read some things that I had written. I did all this reading to educate myself on myself.

I needed to know what I liked and what I didn't like now because things had changed. What was my interest both new and old? I needed to find out what changed that I had let just change without molding, guiding or appreciating. Lord knows I had really just let life happen. I let go of the reins at times on the ride on the road to hell and even close my eyes just hoping I didn't crash. I had a few supporters on the sidelines constantly stirring me in the right direction and encouraging me to not be afraid to hold my head up and look forward.

Besides a small circle of friends from high school, I remained in contact with someone else from my school day that was so unlikely. I remained in contact with my Assistant Principal Mrs. Wilma Holmes Tootle. You see we never really know why someone comes into our lives nor do we know for how long yet I must say; what a blessing she has been!

Mrs. Tootle and her husband Mr. Gerald Tootle have been an amazing support in my life. After my mother passed away I was so lost and distraught. I was a young mother of two and I felt as though my entire world was gone. I felt as though someone wrote my roadmap in disappearing ink and the time for the ink on the paper expired. I was so gone I'd get lost walking in a circle.

Mr. and Mrs. Tootle were there for me if I needed to talk, cry, vent, a ride, a dollar, a meal, a shoulder, an ear, mentors and the list goes on and on and on. They are like another set of parents - "God"parents. I'm so thankful all I can really think to say is "Won't He Do It!!"

Let me elaborate a little. There were times I was hesitant and unsure of what to do even with advice. I didn't think it was something I could do or it wasn't something "for me". See coming from the path I had come from I didn't think that I was going to be allowed to go to college. Single teenage mother, working full time, a full time student and receiving welfare because the monies I made couldn't cover my bills. Nope college cost too much, I'd need books and a babysitter, transportation etc. etc. etc. Me; a college student let alone a graduate was farfetched to say the least in my eyes.

Yet with the amazing support, assistance and encouragement of Mr. and Mrs. Tootle over several years I finally decided to get my degree. I was directed to the perfect school that fit "my" unique and crazy life. I've worked so many jobs in so many different fields; I needed to create several resumes just to submit one to a specific job.

No kidding. The reason being is the work fields I've graced don't even go together. I've worked in a supermarket, I've driven a taxi cab, I work as an office clerk, I worked chiseling barnacles off of Navy ships, a flagger on the dirt roads in the south when road work is being done, I've done hair, Security Officer, Event Planner, Wedding Coordinator, Paraprofessional in the schools, Home health aide, Medical Assistant and Phlebotomist, Accounts Payable & Procurement, Constituent Affairs, Special Events with the parks department, Community Advocacy, Community Service Events, gas station attendant and shift manager, cashier, Actress, writer, stock and inventory person, craft services, production assistant, fast food service, labor and delivery coach, doula and the list goes on and on. So with all that and then some, I had no clue as to what I would wanted to go to school for let alone what I really wanted to do with my life. As I stated I was just pretty much a spectator watching my life happen. I was a drone on autopilot. I was doing whatever was necessary by any means necessary at any time that it was called for.

The phenomenal and unique thing about this school was they allowed me to take all the confusing components of my life and lay them out in such a way it looked like it made a little more sense. I was able to take the knowledge and skills that I learned in the specific jobs and life situations and gain credits for my life experience. I had lived life in such a way that experience was my greatest teacher. Now I was able to apply those teachings to something that seemed to have a little more understanding and meaning to me.

31

In 2009, I registered to SUNY Empire State College located in Old Westbury, NY. It was the best step that I could've taken for myself. SUNY Empire State College, which I will in short refer to as ESC, was life changing.

The faculty and staff are professionals in their own rights. They really know their fields. Not only are the lessons that they teach from the subject in which they are an expert however those lessons many times assisted me in my everyday life. Even the math helped me along the way and Lord knows Statistics was not the easiest thing to work with. Yet it now works in my life with the choices I make and the way I go about making them - go figure.

ESC is not your traditional college experience. Just thinking of being a number amongst 200 people in a class gave me anxiety. There was no way in the hell I would voluntarily put myself through so much stress when my life was already so chaotic. So of course I wanted to run far from the college life.

However, ESC understands that for many adults life has happened and is continuing to happen and that a lot of the experiences we encounter hold a lot of weight as to where we are in life. They have devised a formula that is individualized and structured to the needs and desires of each student. I felt so much like a person that might finally make it. My hope, faith and self-confidence were being recharged and restored.

I was finally on a path whereas I was doing something for me that would make me feel proud of me. Something that was challenging yet in the long run was going to strengthen me mentally and physically. I wasn't doing this for anyone's opinion, anyone person's benefit except my own and that felt amazing. I was challenging myself in a major way.

I was back at being my biggest competition. I was competing with the time in a day as well. 24 hours just wasn't enough. Full time college student, full time internship, part time college federal work study, overtime single parent of 3 girls and grandmother of 2. Nope 24 hours was really not enough time in the day to satisfy everything and everyone. Yet I didn't see Father Time answering my request to go from 24/7 to perhaps 36/9 or something like that, so it was going to be up to me make the changes I needed to make it through this.

I began to schedule and structure things just a little. I knew that I was pretty bad with keeping schedules. However I needed this to work if I was going to get through this process and reach my goal which was to graduate with a degree. I didn't care how long it was going to take I just knew I needed to complete what I started. Completing this process was going to help me to regain my self-understanding about accomplishing tasks and being successful. I needed to prove these things to myself this is what was on my "To Do List".

I found that there were little things I needed to do for me to make my experiences come full circle. I needed to make plans and set goals. Yet even with that I needed to take that a step further. I needed to learn to enjoy the process. When I enjoyed the process I got so much more out of it. When I enjoyed the process it didn't feel like work. When I enjoyed the process it was just that I enjoyed the process; I enjoyed it so much I almost didn't want to get to the end.

Learning and being successful felt so great and amazing that after obtaining my Associate Degree in Advocacy in Human Services in 2011. I registered myself back into school for my Bachelor Degree which I obtained in Health and Healthcare Administration in 2012 from ESC. I was having such a wonderful time during this process I hadn't realized I had so many credits I earned a 4 year degree in 3 years. #WontHeDoIt! That was a challenge I succeeded in that I could hold my head high. For only I know the adversities I had to overcome at the time of this achievement.

While attending ESC, I also did the Federal Work Study (FWS). FWS is a program that gives students the opportunities to work at the college and earn a salary while getting your education. I was able to work right there on the campus I attended. I learned a great deal. I was just soaking up the knowledge and the work experience.

I had the pleasure of working under Mildred Van Burgen and eventually under Samantha James. They are awesome. I was able to assist incoming students with the registration process, prepare documents for admissions, financial aid or faculty. I had the best time doing a multitude of task at ESC. I was finding my place in life and they had no idea just how much they all played a part in where I am today! Thank you a million times Thank You!

During my final year at ESC I applied to the Nassau County Film Commission for an internship they had an open position for. I knew absolutely nothing about film. I just knew I needed to keep busy. I didn't want to stop my flow. I was so use to getting up every day. I was going out and doing something that felt good to me which also benefited me and my family. I was opening myself up to the possibilities that life had in store. I had no idea what they were because I had never ventured down this road before. You know what? I was so okay with that. Call me a thrill seeker or an adrenaline junkie. All I know is that not knowing the unknown began to excite me. It made me want to explore life and experience so much more.

32

So I met the marvelous, kind and huge hearted Debra Markowitz who is the Nassau County Film Commissioner. Debbie is the best at what she does, very resourceful, very knowledgeable and extremely talented. The things I have learned and experienced with and through Debbie are priceless.

The internship gave me another opportunity to challenge myself and learn. I was up for that. I was more than ready! I felt honored that I was being given a chance.

I did an amazing job from what I was told. Hell I was just happy I had somewhere to go every day and do work that was able to help someone out. I learned a great deal about the film industry while I was working there and that was such an additional bonus. Once again experience is the best teacher in my life. So I learned and soaked up as much as I could in the time that I was there.

During the time of my internship Debbie and I became great friends. We talked about work, we talked about films, we talked about family and we talked about health. I knew my health could use some improving. I had let my goal of being a #SizeSatisfied slip out of my sight because I allowed life to happen and I lost focus of me and that goal. It's so easy to lose focus when you have so many things you are trying to accomplish. Yet through our many talks I became refocused and didn't lose sight of anything that I was working on.

I made it mandatory to sit down and prepare a schedule of things to get into the habit of doing. Journaling food, journaling activities, water intake, sleep patterns and things I did throughout the day. After doing this for a while I could see that I needed to be more active, drink more water, eat smaller portions, make better food choices, get better rest and host of other things that I had become blind to. Writing everything down I couldn't deny the facts. It was all right there in front of me in black and white. The truth and nothing but the truth.

Yet where was I going to begin with it this time? Debbie invited me to attend a Weight Watchers meeting. So one day during lunch Debbie and I went to Weight Watchers together. At first I felt awkward and out of place for some of the strangest reasons. People looked older or younger than me, they were already on their way and I felt as though I was just starting, I felt as though I was intruding in on their meetings and I would tell myself I had no money to be spending on trying to learn to eat better. Just as I wanted to quit and had just about talked myself out of it, as a gift, I received a membership for a month or 2 with no out of pocket cost to me. When that happened it seemed to guide my other concerns right out of the window.

My doubts were trying to rent space in my head again. I couldn't let that happen I needed to evict doubt leaving room for confidence, pride and humility. I needed to constantly remind myself of where I'd been and where I wasn't trying to go back to.

I was in a place and a space where I was ready to accept my life and my life choices. I was ready to be real with myself and stop trying to bottle everything up and not discuss it as if it never happened. I was making the conscious decision to make my life an open book. I know that there are many characters that have come across my storyline that have no idea they'd be a part of it. Well guess what Thank You for making my life so very interesting. You've made it all so colorful with the good, the bad and the ugly.

So I took this Weight Watchers experience and ran with it. I went to meetings, I took notes, I tried new foods, I cooked things different, I made better choices and I got better with controlling my portions. I was able to recall all the things I had been learning from Nicolette and Dr. Gadaleta and his team. It may sound a little weird however I ate more frequently however the meals were a lot smaller. Instead of 3 large meals throughout the day I had 4-6 small meals throughout the day with plenty of water and healthier snack choices in between. I also added B12 sublingual vitamins, Chromium Picolinate, multivitamins and calcium supplements to my daily routine as well.

Things finally began to look like they were making a little bit of sense and ultimately becoming full circle. I was beginning not to feel so lost and confused. I was finally getting back comfortable in my own life and in my own skin. I felt like I was getting a better understanding of myself. I was not only building this newfound respect and relationship with food eventually it was also with me; go figure. I was amazed and astonished at how much I learned about me through my relationship with food. It was so not a good one. This change and insight was much needed.

See what I found out when I starting speaking with different people and really listening. I realized that this struggle wasn't mine alone. Some people have this "thing" as to where anything they do they tend to make it look easy. Prime example I see someone from high school that I haven't seen in years and they would say hey long time no see, boy you've changed. And those words would come with a look of "oh how you've grown not only up however more so you've grown out..." I'm smart. I can read between the lines very well.

I on the other hand would tell people I was working on losing my baby fat. They would say awwww and ask how old was the baby and I'd tell them 10. Yeah yeah I know how pitiful. Yet it was the truth and I was being serious. I found myself making light of my imperfections before anyone else could. Half the time I had no idea if I was going to be the butt of the joke or not so I was already with my own punchlines. This only sharpened my sarcasm being able to guard myself, making my best offense my defense.

I was so thankful to Debbie for inviting me to go with her to Weight Watchers. Not that I believed she needed to go. I would just take it that she was there to support me and that made me feel great. Her energy is amazing and her soul forever smiles on others. We spoke about energy, the Universe and other topics that made me feel good to take the information in.

At Weight Watchers they had some of the best staff. They were very concerned, caring and passionate people. There were so many that I came across however there are two that really left their impression in my life forever. I must say a special thank you to Sandy and Jackie. Plus having Jennifer Hudson as their face and seeing her life transformations made me feel so inspired and motivated to do the same. So if anyone reads this that knows Jennifer Hudson please tell her I humbly thank her for sharing her story.

33

I attended the Weight Watchers center in Carle Place, NY and that is where Jackie was the greeter and cashier or support staff and Sandy was the Meeting Leader. They really loved their jobs and what they were doing. They are so passionate about the work they do. There were times I could be bought to tears coming to a meeting getting on the scale to find out I'm up a pound or 10. When I felt as though I was failing and just wanted to retreat to a hole with a pint of ice cream, some chips and 2 liter of soda Jackie and Sandy would encourage me to sit and just listen if nothing else. That was sometimes all I needed.

Hearing the struggles, sacrifices, achievements, goals and awkward moments of others told me that I'm not alone. Even still I wasn't ready to start sharing my story. I felt as though nothing I would say could be understood by anyone and the things that I was struggling with were embarrassing. However after a short while I took the chance to chime in and I felt so supported and no longer afraid to share. I thanked them all because even though I had not said much I had left many meetings with much. I gained tips about exercises, recipes, new foods and having a new perspective on many things regarding food, weight and life. Wow, all that by just being there and listening, I received some jewels.

I got to the point where I realized that I needed a better budget because the budget of mine that I already had had a budget that needed to get a budget. Yup the story of my life, I am always juggling things like a circus clown. My eye hand coordination is impeccable. I mean many times I would find myself wearing more hats than a wig store has Styrofoam heads. Never ending battle, there's a constant tug of war with me getting things right. I felt as though nothing would ever be normal. Then I realized is there truly such a thing as normal? What exactly is normal anyway?

As people we need to realize that we cannot run from our problems. The problems are within us they are a part of who we are and where we go they go. There are sensory triggers that may cause these things to resurface regardless of how far you think you may have "run" from something. A sound, a statement, a voice, a song, a smell, a touch, a tone, a sight there are so many things. Virtually anything can do it. You can't stop being or existing in the world, so you have to learn how to one by one start dealing with issues and finding solutions. Sort through your life and your reality. Don't lose yourself in someone else's reality trying to run from your own. Just reinvent yourself by molding the you that you have found yourself to be. When positive changes take place you have to feed the fire and feed off of that positive energy. Just as when things were going wrong and you feed into the negative you gave the negative power. It's time to feel the power of positivity. I challenge you to feed into that and let me know what happens. Be consistent and watch the habits you form.

My life is so amazing. My journey and my process have been so profound. I am still a work in progress on many levels. I have faith and I will not give up on me. I know how determined and hard I can go for a person, for a cause for anything so why don't I deserve to do the same if not more for me.

I dug in deep. Some things I had to touch really hurt. Not touching them where like letting a scar heal and tearing off the scab continuously. Which was a more permanent solution to healing? Facing myself, my fears and my issues dead on, with an open mind and honestly or trying to run and avoid the inevitable. Regardless of the result I was ready, willing and open for different results. I am the captain of my ship and I am ready to go off into unchartered waters.

34

I am now currently working in the local county parks department. I do things in the parks department that are so diversified that my job keeps me well rounded and never bored. From accounts payable, special events, ordering farm animal food and constituent affairs the day can consist of anything.

I've been blessed since working my way to a #SizeSatisfied to doing some modeling projects. That in itself was a leap out on faith. See let me explain. Before losing weight if you were able to get me in a picture you were so lucky. Taking pictures was not something I liked to do. Hell they say it added 10 pounds and I knew I needed to lose at least 40 pounds before you'd catch a snap shot. So therefore "we" (me, myself and I) refrained from any and all photo opportunities.

This takes me back to Debbie. Debbie is beyond amazing as I stated before. Allow me to elaborate a tad bit more as to why. I mentioned that I worked as an intern with Debbie. After I left and began working at the parks department, Debbie and I remained in touch as we had a built a wonderful friendship. She had received a submission notice from the now hit series Orange Is The New Black on Netflix. They were looking for African American females in my age range with tattoos to portray inmates. She reached out to me and suggested that I submit my info and a picture or two to them. I respectfully declined because I wasn't one to take pictures let alone film in front of a camera. I felt wonderful that she had thought I'd be good enough for it I just didn't agree. She asked me to really consider it and told me I should give it a shot.

A day or so went by and she followed up with me. I told her I had not done anything and she continued to encourage me. So I figured that if I was rewriting my story why not do something I had never done before. The worst thing that could happen is they didn't want me. So I decided to submit my information and I emailed them. To my surprise they contacted me in less than an hour by phone. They say if you want something you've never had you have to do things you've never done.

I received a phone call from this sweet casting agent named Ro. She was so pleasant. She told me that the director and writer wanted to know if I would be available to come in for an interview. An interview? I didn't understand. I thought I was only submitting for a role as background talent. Why would I need to be interviewed for that? So I asked could I call her back and immediately called Debbie with concern, excitement and nervousness surging through my body.

Debbie was so excited when I told her what they said. She supported and encouraged me to follow through and to go for it. I trust Debbie so I did. I called Ro back and made the appointment for the interview. This was one of the first major steps I was taking on this new found road on my life. I was excited, nervous, anxious, prepared for the unknown and ready for anything.

I arrived at the studio feeling like a leaf on a tree during a hurricane. Yet I was going to see this part of this process through. I had made it this far so why not take the next step forward. I sign in, I take a seat and I wait to be called into the interview.

They came out and they called me. The walk to the room felt like a hike in itself. Knees shaking like I was walking a tightrope for the first time with no safety net. We finally arrive I shake hands, introduce myself and have a seat. The rest from there was smooth sailing and as easy as a conversation. Why? Because that's exactly what it turned into a friendly honest conversation.

They asked questions. I answered. We laughed. It was great! I left the interview feeling incredible. Later that evening I received the call that they wanted to have me on the show. They even wanted to have me as part of a featured gang that was going to be on the show. I was ecstatic. I didn't know what to do with myself. I was overjoyed and so very thankful. Life was surprising me and once again finally starting to look up.

I contacted Debbie to share the phenomenal news. I couldn't thank her enough. I also told her about being offered a waiver for my work on the show. I had no idea what that meant or what it was for, apparently it was a great thing though; is what I later found out.

I was blessed to be asked by production to film for four days. That was four of the best days of my life. On a TV set with actors, actresses, writers, PAs, directors, producers, lights, cameras and a language all its own, absolutely breathtaking moments. I was floored. I was bit by the bug and ready to do dive in head first into acting and the film industry.

I went to a casting agency and registered myself with them for work. I created an online profile and became my own booking agent. I was going to learn this business and process. I was determined to do it well. I was determined and focused on the task at hand. I saw something that I wanted and I was going to go after it. That's right I wanted it and I was going to get it. The fire inside me was lit. They say fake it till you make it, guess what truth be told I've been doing that most of my life.

After completing my time on Orange Is The New Black my next project was a movie with Danny Glover entitled Back In The Day. I was then introduced to the world of Independent Films or Indies for short. The more I learned the more I fell in love.

I got to work on this extremely creative dramedy (drama comedy), written and directed by the talented Debra Markowitz. This project truly introduced me to the film industry. I learned about being a part of the cast and production crew. I learned about credits, union and nonunion, call sheets, location management, craft services, assistant director, the duties of a PA (production Assistant) and the list goes on and on and on and on. I also worked on By Blood written and directed by Debbie. Plus I've done a host of other projects that I have held dear to my heart. I love film!

35

Within this process of learning in a new field I continued to learn more about myself. I was able to sharpen the skills I already had, learn new skills and sort through some of my life likes and dislikes. Since this was my life and my process I didn't have to allow any outside forces or people to deter me from what I thought best fit me. Whether it be my trial and errors or it be my trials and my triumphs; either way they were mine and mine alone.

So I took in all this knowledge and these lessons and decided that I wanted to know more and do more in the filming industry. As I continued to rewrite my story, go through the process of life and find myself. I realized just like anything else that I have ever practiced; I learned I could become a master of my own life. All I needed to do was give myself the desired and required amount of space and time to deal with the things that my life entailed. The only time I needed to take outside advice on my life was when I chose to. Not simply take it or deal with it because it was imposed or offered. I had to take time to know what was best for me.

Knowing that I was now going to be doing some things in life that put me not only in front and behind the camera but also in the sight of many others including myself; the question became what is it that I want to see? What is the image of me that I feel is appealing? So I made a commitment to myself to not just go on a diet or to lose weight however I committed to live a healthier, happier more positive lifestyle. I wasn't doing this for a season. I was doing this for a reason and that reason was me.

I was going to make time for me. Time for me to eat right, time for me to workout, time for me to relax, time for me to center myself and regroup when needed, time for me and whatever it was that that time was needed for. I was in a committed relationship with myself and I am the faithful type. The schedule, the meals, the rest and relaxation that I took for myself was outstanding. I felt and still feel epic. I am at a place in my life that I never ever knew existed.

Through the love I have for myself, others seem to have an abundance of love and respect for me. I set the tone for how others receive me and treat me. I will not tolerate or accept anything less. I set the boundaries and the standards that those who are in my circle need to know to follow. You have to do the same. When you don't set boundaries, people don't know their limits. Be the conductor of your orchestra, you set the tone and flow of your melody.

While looking to find myself, I had to dig and dig deep. I had to face things that I wanted to forget, I have had to take steps when I would rather run, I had to shape up or ship out literally. I had to move when I would've preferred to be still, I had to think positive when in the midst of negative, I had to practice and train myself to learn and utilize my new found skills constantly, I had to do a lot and I still am. I'm so not perfect yet I am perfecting myself. I've had to open myself up to change and not try to determine every aspect of that change. I've had to learn to trust and to love again.

There are some people that may not know that I love them because my negative vibes controlled my tongue and my actions when I was in their presence. Perhaps I could've taken a minute or two to look at things in another perspective so that the conclusion we came to could've been more of a compromise. For my part and anything that I lacked I take this time to sincerely apologize.

36

My journey to my #SizeSatisfied took me to nooks and crevasses in my life that I was unaware existed. This journey not only shaped me physically however also mentally, emotionally and spiritually. My journey has been a renewing and reinventing process. I am so in tune and in touch with myself and that feels amazing. I have taken the time to know myself, what I want and where I am going. Visions that I have are so impeccable. I'm floored with awe.

If a young girl such as me from a small town called Glen Cove, NY with obstacles and issues by the barrels can find herself amongst all the muck and the mud. Know that you should not give up! Give yourself the chance that you deserve. Treat yourself like a new friend and be sure to get much acquainted. I bet you will find some interesting things out about yourself. You will either embrace the changes, develop them or you will find yourself tweaking it to the change that you yourself need.

I have shed the weight of my worries and lost a whole person in the process. Great Mental, Physical, Emotional and Spiritual health are all essential. You cannot take care of one without the other. Our thoughts stir up feelings, bringing life to our thoughts turning thoughts into actions that leave us with feelings about our thoughts and the cycle continues. Be sure to filter your cycle. Work on keeping it positive and pure. Do a little spring cleaning. Change happens every moment of everyday. Know that the consistency, longevity and communication you develop with yourself will lead to the response you get from others.

No one is perfect. No one is the same. Be yourself. Know that your imperfections are your trademarks. They can never be copy written or patented. You own that. So be sure to present the best of you in all you do. Be confident. Be bold. Be You.

This has been my journey to my #SizeSatisfied thus far. I am a #WorkInProgress.

#GodIsntFinishedWithMeYet.

The #Universe still has so much to share. Since I know that life is always happening I know this isn't the final chapter.

37

Sample Solutions to My #SizeSatisfied

Meal Sample Plan:

Half hour before eating hydrate: drink water

*Breakfast Option #1: Morning coffee flavored with 2
Splendas and creamer
2 eggs any style
Whole grain toast
Fruit*

*Breakfast Option #2: Oatmeal with fresh fruit and
cinnamon sprinkle a little brown sugar if you choose
for sweetness*

Hydrate: Drink Water

*Midmorning snack: yogurt with nuts or granola and
fruit*

Hydrate: Drink Water

*Lunch Option #1: Chopped salad with sweet butter
lettuce or mixed greens and spinach
Blackened chicken
Black beans
Roasted sweet corn
Carrots*

Boiled eggs
Gorgonzola cheese
With Balsamic Vinaigrette

Lunch Option #2: Sushi and Miso soup
Or
1 specialty slice of pizza and a ginger ale

Hydrate: Drink Water

Midday snack: ½ cup of trail mix or mixed nuts

Hydrate: Drink Water

Dinner Option #1: Grilled chicken breast (skinless and boneless)
14 cup Sautéed spinach with garlic and chopped onions
Oven roasted baby carrots and broccoli

Dinner Option#2: Teriyaki Oven baked salmon
Oven roasted Brussel sprouts with string beans and cubed potatoes

Late night snack: frozen grapes and frozen raspberries
Hydrate: Drink Water

Honestly I followed no exact same plan. I just made sure to incorporate plenty of proteins, fruits, vegetables, and water into my daily intake. I cut down own my intake of carbs and sweets. I basically became mindful of the food I was eating and taking notes on the amount of motion I need to create.

When it first came to working out I would find every excuse in the book as to why I couldn't work out right now. I was always tied up and busy doing something or nothing. Perhaps I was just busy thinking about it. Either way that wasn't gonna cut it.

Because I was new to exercising I had to work my way up to it. At first I would only do it in the privacy of my room when no one was home because I thought I looked funny and I didn't want to have to answer any questions or be laughed at. So I did things like arm rotations, leg lifts, squats, lunges, dips off the edge of the bed, pushups off the bed or a chair - basically I did anything I could that made me feel like I was making a difference.

Trust me I know you all must be like but I'm watching my favorite show. So what! Then guess what that is why they have commercials. Use that 2.2 minutes to start the change of your lifetime. As you do this more and more it will become routine. You will find that you want to venture out and add other activities and areas to your work out. That's great! Walk in the park or around the block, if you have stairs in your house make a variety of exercises that you incorporate them into for a routine for the core, legs and arms.

The things that one can do to workout are endless. You do not always need a gym. You can utilize things at home as well as your own body to get the resistance and weight that you need for that session. Be creative. There is no right or wrong workout to choose unless you just choose just not to work out! The more you move, the more you lose.

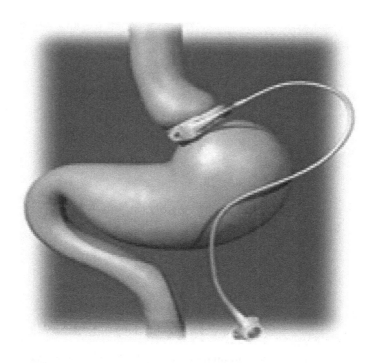

LAPBAND
http://bariatric.stopobesityforlife.com/obesity-surgery/correcting-obesity/procedures/laparoscopic-sleeve-gastrectomy-gastric-sleeve-surgery/

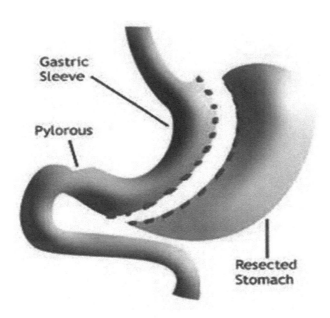

GASTRIC SLEEVE

NOTES

NOTES

NOTES

Acknowledgements

I'd like to Thank and acknowledge all those that have supported and encouraged me on my journey of transformation. I'd like to thank all my children and grandchildren for their patience and support as I have worked diligently on this project. Okay patience perhaps not so much. Continuously kicking them out and sometimes ignoring their calls for refereeing debates and situations.

I must Thank the Universe and the Man upstairs for the courage and wisdom to complete this book.

To LaTosha Capone I must Thank you first and for most for pointing me in the proper direction to complete this book and publish it! Thank you Thank you Thank you!!

I would also like to Thank Mr. and Mrs. Tootle for being there for me during my times of life's down times and times of hardship as well as encouraging me and inspiring me to always see that things can be better. I thank you for being the example that I needed on so many levels. You two have been parents to a parentless child. You are absolutely amazing and you have done an outstanding job if I may say so myself.

To my best friend and sister Danica Jackson for being there with me on nights that I cried, nights that I laughed, nights that I cooked and some nights that I couldn't. I appreciate the times of getting absolutely twisted off of coffee and cake and waking up as if we fell asleep at the bar (you just had to be there)!

To my circle of sisters that have been there with me since high school; Careen Magee, Amber Lyons, Venus Ramos, Siadely Concepcion and Gladys Perez thank you thank you thank you for just being there.
To ALL those that continue to inspire and encourage me I say thank you to too!

Without question or hesitation I'd like to THANK all those that ever told me No, denied me help, closed their doors on me, turned their backs on me, disrespected me, abused me, bullied me, told me I couldn't do it, told me I'd amount to nothing, took advantage of me, hoped and prayed I would fail, stole from me, try to use me as a negative example, thought I was out of my mind and my league. You made me stronger in ways you I hope you never have to understand yet know I am ever so grateful for you too.

I also would like to send a very special THANK YOU to Mr. Junius Dean Godboldo for sitting down with me and encouraging me to sit down and share my story. Mr. Dean you are greatly appreciated. You left a lot for me to think about in such a short time. You are a wealth of knowledge. Your passion for all things is infectious. Thank you, thank you, and thank you!! You and your family made me feel so welcome in your home. I am so appreciative of that. Much LOVE and RESPECT to you all. Continue to build memories that will outlive this lifetime.

To Cliffton "Clipperman" Godboldo I must extend a deep heartfelt THANK YOU to you for all the late night talks about life and reality. For talking me off a ledge when you never even really knew that I was on one. For being a lifesaver with comedy that cures. It ales and aides in times of distress. For our intense talks about choices and perception. Your comfort and support was the best that a friend or anyone could ever visualize. You are a blessing to all that you touch with your talent and your words. The Universe has just as much in store for you as it had for the world when it presented you into it. Much thanks to Mr. Junius Dean Godboldo and Mrs. Carol Godboldo :)... Thank you Thank you and Thank you!!

To my Notorious 21 MC family everywhere I truly appreciate you all ~ both past and present! DEUCE ONE!

To my Sophisticated family I love you all!

As for medical staff that has made my steps a little easier and literally a little lighter. You made sure that I was well informed, you supported and encouraged my decisions, they gave me time when I wasn't sure and provided me with the best care that I could've imagined. I was presented with options with clear and precise information. To the bariatric team of Dr. Dominick Gadaleta, Yvonne, Carol and the amazing office and surgical team. To the medical staff at the North Shore LIJ Hospital located in Manhasset, NY, Charmaine, the Pre-surgical department, Admissions, PAC Department through discharge; you were all such caring inspiring professionals. Thank you! To Dr. Dominick Riina thank you for guiding me in the right direction when I believed that I was ready to just get liposuction, then give up because I couldn't lose the weight, continue to consult with me when other doctors wouldn't help and being the professional with an amazing heart, talent and skill. Thank you Thank you Thank you!

Special thanks to Nicolette Pace the amazing caring nutritionist that helped me touch the root of some of my eating anchors. Nicolette you allowed me to be myself and with that I required honesty and time. Both things I was unfamiliar with yet it was time for change. Thank you for knowing that all things are connected and for touching me with our many talks.

In addition I need to thank my educational facilitators. My professors at SUNY Empire State College at the Old Westbury Campus Thank you. You ALL are professionals and experts in your selected fields. Your ingenuity gives your students the chance to look at things in alternative perspectives and leave room for broader perception of all things. You ensured that the lessons you taught in the classrooms could be utilized not only in the classroom however also throughout life. Thank you!

I have to extend a warm heartfelt and deep rooted thank you to Debra Markowitz. You opened your office up to me and you gave me a chance. I had the best internship known to man. This was an internship that blossomed into the most beautiful friendship. I am ever so thankful to you and the powers of the Universe. We know that everything happens for a reason and when I first can to your office I had no idea why I was there. However look at the direction destiny has pointed me in and it was through you! You changed my life and I am ever so thankful to you for so many things! Opportunities, Networking connections, knowledge, direction, love, chances, skills, knowledge, Weight Watchers, an awesome personal trainer :) etc etc etc the list could go on forever and ever! Thank you from the bottom of my soul! You saw things in me when I could even connect with me. Your sincerity and passion are infectious!

I would like to thank Sandy and Jackie at Weight Watchers in Carle Place, NY.

Thank you Ecindy Stein, Maryola Dannebaum and Michael Law for the amazing photo shoots. I truly appreciate you. You helped me to see myself in a different light. I can't wait to work with you all again.

I'd like to thank Sara Klima for being an amazing personal trainer and putting up with my crazy schedule and chaotic life.

I know that there are so many more medical staff, nutritionist, weight watchers staff and members, gym staff, personal trainers, friends and so many others to thank! Please know that I THANK YOU ALL FROM THE BOTTOM OF MY SOUL!! Please charge my mind and not my heart!!

#ForeverMovingForward

#WorkInProgress

Finding My Way
To
A
#BetterMe

&

A
#SizeSatisfied

My Journey to a
#SizeSatisfied
&
Finding Myself In the Process
Losing the Weight of My Worries

Synopsis

This is for all those that struggle with finding their way to a healthier You. As well as to those who just struggle to make their life better. No matter your struggle you can overcome it with practice and patience. I know that sounds easier said than done, however I know if I can; you can. I am going to tell you some things about me in this book that took me through the ups, the downs, the ins and outs as well as the twists and turns of my journey. Things that made me who I am today. The good, the bad and the indifferent. Regardless of what the circumstances, the hurdles or the challenges I encountered I know that I wouldn't change a thing.

I hope this supports someone so that they know they are not alone. I hope this inspires someone with direction if they weren't sure which way to go. I want to share my journey because I am sure that it is not my path alone. I followed footsteps along the way until I could make my own and I left a set of footprints for others to follow until you find the path that best fits You. All I ask is you pay it forward and do the same for someone you know or don't know. Just once you've made your way and achieved a goal, I ask that you help and guide someone else to that amazing feeling of success.

This in no way serves as a replacement for a professional medical consultation. This is just me sharing my story of my journey so far. Forty years and counting... I'm not finished with my journey. I am a work in progress.

If you need support, recipes, fitness ideas or challenges please come follow me and reach out:

Come join the
#SizeSatisfied Movement
It's not for a minute it's for a Lifetime!!

Please follow me on Instagram at:
Cautionn21

Friend me and follow me on Facebook at:
Regina Caution Hardy
or
Regina MzExtremeCaution Hardy

And

Follow Me On Twitter at:
@ExtremeCaution